MICROSOFT® *Quick* REFERENCE

W9-AWN-770

HARD DISK
MANAGEMENT

Second Edition

INCLUDES
DOS 5

Microsoft
P R E S S ®

VAN WOLVERTON

PUBLISHED BY
Microsoft Press
A Division of Microsoft Corporation
One Microsoft Way
Redmond, Washington 98052-6399

Library of Congress Cataloging-in-Publication Data
Wolverton, Van, 1939–
    Hard disk management / Van Wolverton. -- 3rd ed.
        p.   cm. -- (Microsoft quick reference)
    Includes index.
    ISBN 1-55615-351-1
    1. Hard disk management.   I. Title.   II. Series.
QA76.9.H35W65 1991
004.5'6--dc20   90-24930
                                                    CIP

Printed and bound in the United States of America.

2 3 4 5 6 7 8 9   MLML   4 3 2 1

Distributed to the book trade in Canada by Macmillan of Canada,
a division of Canada Publishing Corporation.

Distributed to the book trade outside the United States and Canada
by Penguin Books Ltd.

Penguin Books Ltd., Harmondsworth, Middlesex, England
Penguin Books Australia Ltd., Ringwood, Victoria, Australia
Penguin Books N.Z. Ltd., 182–190 Wairau Road, Auckland 10,
New Zealand

British Cataloging-in-Publication Data available.

Project Editor: JoAnne Woodcock
Technical Editor: Jim Johnson

Contents

Introduction

A hard disk can hold far more data than a diskette can, and DOS, the disk manager, can move files to and from a hard disk much more quickly than it can move files to and from a diskette. As its name implies, a hard disk isn't flexible like a diskette; typically, data is recorded on one or more rigid metal platters enclosed in a sealed case. A hard disk is also frequently called a fixed disk. Again, as this name implies, you don't remove a fixed disk — it is permanently fixed in the drive.

Because a hard disk can hold so many more files than a diskette, using it effectively requires more planning and housekeeping than using diskettes does. A hard disk also benefits from a little more care and routine maintenance too, and for the same reason: because you entrust so many of your programs and so much of your data to it.

Although a hard disk eliminates the inconvenience of swapping diskettes, and although you spend much less time waiting for DOS to find a file or copy it to memory, you have to invest some time in planning how you'll organize your files and in keeping the disk orderly.

It's not unlike keeping track of paper files. When all you have are a couple of dozen file folders with a few sheets of paper in each, you can keep all the files on your desktop. This approach can get aggravating, however, when you have a lot of bulky files and you have to shuffle in and among them, searching for what you want.

Switching to a file cabinet gives you more room for files and cleans up your desktop, but if you don't set up some sort of filing system with dividers, hanging file folders, and labeled manila folders, finding the files you need becomes even harder. And when the drawers start filling up — as they always do — you have to go through and thin out the files, tossing the ones you no longer need and putting those you might need later into a storage box, and hoping as you go that you haven't discarded when you should have saved.

So it is with computer files, especially when you use a hard disk and several application programs. Files proliferate, and it's all too easy to lose track of the ones you need or to throw out some you should have kept. But properly organized and managed, a hard disk lets you work significantly faster, with a minimum of fuss.

Many tools are available for managing this capacious filing cabinet. Some are as close at hand as your DOS prompt; others come from independent providers of hardware and software. Because this reference is not intended as a buyer's guide and because disk-management needs vary with the ways in which hard disks are used, this book concentrates on DOS commands designed for hard disk management. In particular, this guide focuses on the disk-management, file-management, and data-protection features of version 5 of DOS, but the book is appropriate for earlier versions, too. That's because newer versions of DOS remain compatible with older versions even as they incorporate new features to help make your work easier. Thus, much of this book applies as easily to version 3 as it does to version 5.

WHAT'S IN THIS QUICK REFERENCE

Throughout this book, the emphasis is on the two tasks that are more important than any others in managing your hard disk efficiently: setting up your filing system and protecting both your hard disk and your data files. This book doesn't cover the basics of using DOS; it assumes that you know what DOS is and how to use its commands. Instead, it focuses on the commands and techniques that let you take advantage of the hard disk's capacity and speed. Much of the material is taken from two other Microsoft Press books,

Running MS-DOS and *Supercharging MS-DOS;* the information is selected and either edited or expanded to provide the most relevant information on hard disk management in this smaller, more convenient format.

- Part I, "How a Hard Disk Works," briefly describes how a hard disk stores information and how DOS finds the files it needs on a hard disk.

- Part II, "Preparing Your Hard Disk," describes how you install DOS on your hard disk and, if necessary, use the Fdisk, Format, Setup, and Copy commands to identify the hard disk to DOS and prepare it for use.

- Part III, "Configuring DOS for Your Hard Disk," describes the configuration commands you should include in the file named CONFIG.SYS to make the best use of your hard disk. It also includes some techniques you can use to tailor your system to the hard disk.

- Part IV, "Working with Directories," describes the commands you use to set up your filing system and tell DOS where you keep your command and data files.

- Part V, "Working with Files," describes the DOS commands you use to manage your files, emphasizing those that let you deal with the large number of files a hard disk can hold.

- Part VI, "Protecting Your Hard Disk," describes the commands you use to safeguard the information stored on your hard disk. These include commands that back up and restore files, maintain an up-to-date file that saves information on the current status of the hard disk, and can even reverse the effects of formatting a hard disk.

- Part VII, "Maintaining Your Hard Disk," suggests some ways you can keep your hard disk running.

- Part VIII, "Using the DOS Shell," shows you how to use the version 5 DOS Shell to accomplish many disk-management tasks without having to type commands at the system prompt.

WHAT TO TYPE AND WHEN

This quick reference uses the following conventions to distinguish what you do from how your computer responds:

- Hands-on examples are shown in a different typeface, on separate lines, just as you would see them on your display. The characters you type are shaded. For example,

```
C:\>path
PATH=C:\;C:\DOS;C:\WORD;C:\EXCEL
```

- Occasionally, similar information appears in the text. In these instances, the interaction between you and the computer is printed in italics to distinguish it from the surrounding text. For example, "If you type *path* to display the command path, but no command path is defined, DOS responds *No path*."

- The names of keys are shown as they appear on your keyboard. The only exceptions are the direction keys—they are called Up, Down, Left, and Right. If you must press two or more keys simultaneously, the key names are connected with hyphens; Ctrl-Break, for example, means hold down the Ctrl key and press the Break key.

- The examples usually include the current directory as part of the system prompt—for example, C:\DOS>. Your display will be different if the current drive isn't drive C or if you have defined your own system prompt.

- Many commands include parameters that let you specify a drive letter, a file, or another variable. These parameters are shown in italics to indicate that they represent a variable entry. When you must enter a parameter exactly, it is shown in the form you must use. For example,

```
path pathname ;
```

The word *path* and the semicolon are required and must be entered as shown. The variable *pathname* represents the path name of a directory; you must add this.

PART I

How a Hard Disk Works

Information is stored on a disk much as music or video is recorded on magnetic tape. A brief description of how a hard disk is organized and how DOS uses it can help you understand the commands you use to manage it.

TYPES OF HARD DISK

Hard disks come in different sizes and shapes. Most common is the internal drive, which is installed inside the system unit of your computer, usually beneath or beside the diskette drive. Several other types are available:

- A "hard disk on a card" fits inside the system unit but is mounted on a printed-circuit card that plugs into a socket on the main circuit board, rather than being installed adjacent to the diskette drive.

- An external drive is housed in its own case outside the system unit. It is connected to the computer by cables through which data and control signals pass, and it usually has its own power cord.

- Some hard disk drives, both internal and external, have removable cartridges that you can store and exchange as you do diskettes.

All these hard disk drives operate in much the same way; regardless of the type you have, you use the same techniques and commands to manage the hard disk.

Note: One type of disk drive, called the Bernoulli Box, has the capacity and speed of a hard disk but is really a special type of diskette sealed in a removable cartridge. Although you generally treat it as you would a hard disk, there are a few special considerations; if you use a Bernoulli Box, check its documentation for any exceptions to the information in this book.

INSIDE A HARD DISK

A hard disk of the sort shown in Figure 1-1 contains two or more thin metal platters, either 3½ or 5¼ inches in diameter, stacked on a central axis, or spindle. A separate arm holds a series of read/write heads, one head for each surface of each platter. An electric motor turns the spindle, rotating the platters so that they move past the heads.

The platters are coated with a magnetic material similar to the coating on audio and video tape, so that information can be written to (recorded on) or read (played back) from the disk. This entire assembly, including the motor and the recording heads, is sealed in an airtight case.

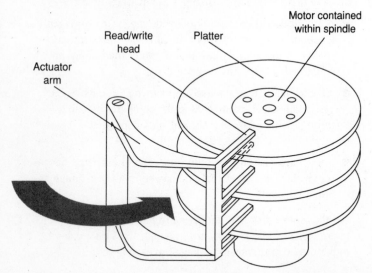

Figure 1-1. *A simplified drawing of the inside of a hard disk drive.*

Two factors give a hard disk greater storage capacity than a diskette:

- A hard disk drive contains more than one magnetically coated disk.

- Data can be recorded much more densely because the drive unit is enclosed in an airtight enclosure, the platters and magnetic coating are more finely machined, and the drive heads are smaller and closer to the platters.

The storage capacity of typical diskettes used on MS-DOS computers ranges from 160 KB to 2.88 MB. Hard disk capacities generally range from 20 MB to 110 MB, with 30 MB to 60 MB the most frequently used sizes. Much larger units are becoming more common; hard disks for the IBM PS/2 Model 80, for example, can hold as much as 314 MB, and third-party manufacturers offer hard disks for IBM-compatible computers with capacities of 760 MB and more.

SIDES, TRACKS, AND SECTORS

Just as on a diskette, data is stored on the platters of a hard disk in narrow concentric circles called tracks. Each track is divided into segments called sectors; a sector typically holds 512 bytes. Each platter, of course, has two sides. These sides, tracks, and sectors are physical portions of the hard disk.

Figure 1-2 on the following page shows how tracks and sectors are laid out on one side of a hard disk platter. For simplicity, the illustration shows only four tracks, each divided into nine sectors. A hard disk has more tracks than this, and each track is divided into more sectors, but the pattern is the same. The exact number of tracks and sectors varies, depending on the hard disk's capacity.

When DOS formats a hard disk, it numbers each side, track, and sector. When DOS stores a file on the disk, it stores the location of the beginning of a file in the file's directory entry. The Directory command doesn't display this information, but DOS can find any sector on a disk by

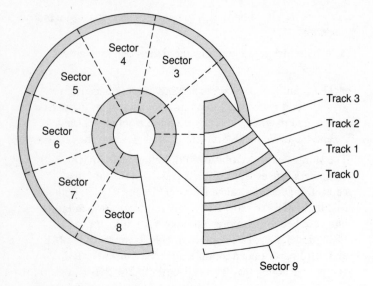

Figure 1-2. *Tracks and sectors on a disk.*

its side, track, and sector numbers, just as you can find any seat in a stadium or a theater by its section, row, and seat numbers.

But in most cases you don't have to deal with these platters and their sides, tracks, and sectors; true, they're part of the hard disk drive, but with rare exceptions all you need to know about are drive letters, path names, and file names.

Note: In some versions, DOS uses the term *cylinder* when referring to a disk (for example, in response to the Fdisk and Format commands). A cylinder is made up of all the tracks with the same number on each side of each platter. If a hard disk has three platters, for example, cylinder 5 consists of the "stack" formed by the six tracks numbered 5 on the upper and lower surfaces of the three platters.

HOW DOS STORES FILES

When you format a disk, DOS lays out a certain pattern of tracks and sectors on it. The sectors are like empty storage compartments, each capable of holding a fixed number of bytes. For file storage, DOS clumps sectors into larger units called *clusters,* each of which can be used to hold a portion of a file. For each file it stores, DOS then uses as many clusters as it needs, placing part of the file in each cluster. These clusters—groups of consecutive sectors— are not necessarily in consecutive locations on the disk surface. In fact, they often are not.

To find the various parts of a file once it's been stored on disk, DOS uses a device called a File Allocation Table, or FAT (pronounced "fat"). This FAT is a linked list, or chain, in which each link tells DOS where to find the next cluster—the next part of the disk—in which the file is stored.

You don't have to know or worry about clusters and the FAT any more than you have to concern yourself with the mechanical parts of your hard disk. If you have version 5 of DOS, however, passing familiarity with these terms is useful because this version of DOS includes Undelete, Unformat, and Quick Format commands that are easier to understand if you know about the FAT than if you don't.

A HARD DISK VOCABULARY

If your computer already has a hard disk and you're per- fectly satisfied with it, you probably don't care what its ac- cess time is, what the interleave is, or how it encodes data. If you're about to buy a computer, however, or if you're planning to add a hard disk to your system, you'll probably encounter a few new terms when you go shopping. A com- plete explanation is beyond the scope of this small book, but to help you get your bearings, here are some brief definitions:

■ Disk controller. Every hard disk and diskette drive, ex- cept a hard disk on a card, needs one of these. It's a printed-circuit card that provides a link between your computer and the drive mechanism, just as a video adapter links the system with your display.

■ Access time. This is the amount of time it takes for the drive to position the read/write heads over the disk and transfer information in response to a read or write request. Currently, an access time of less than 30 milliseconds is fast; less than 20 milliseconds is really fast.

■ Interleave. This is a ratio, such as 3:1 or 1:1, that tells you how many sectors fall between two sectors that the hard disk reads or writes consecutively on a track. Now what does that mean? Simply that the platters in a hard disk spin so fast (several thousand times per minute) that sectors fly under the read/write heads faster than some drives can read from or write to them. To eliminate this mismatch, "consecutive" sectors on the disk are actually separated physically. A 3:1 interleave, for example, means there are two sectors between each one DOS uses in sequence. A 1:1 interleave means the sectors are used sequentially. The more efficient the disk, the less separation between "consecutive" sectors it requires.

■ Disk transfer speed or data transfer rate. This is the speed at which information can be transferred to and from the disk and your computer's memory.

■ MFM, RLL, IDE, ESDI, and other types of encoding. These acronyms tell you the method used by the hard disk for encoding data as changes in magnetic polarity on the surface of the disk platters. If you're buying a hard disk, be sure the disk controller and the hard disk use the same encoding method.

INSTALLING A HARD DISK

If the hard disk comes as part of the computer system, the dealer should install the hard disk, prepare it, format it, and—if you buy DOS at the same time—install DOS on it. The service personnel at most stores are professionals; they'll install the drive quickly and correctly, and they'll test it to be sure it works.

If the dealer charges extra for this service, either pay the price or go to a dealer who doesn't charge for it. If your dealer won't install the drive or won't guarantee the system, find one who will.

If you're adding a hard disk to your computer, be sure the unit will fit into your system and operate correctly with other disk drives you have. For example, if you're buying a second hard disk, check to be certain that your first will work with it, and vice versa.

Once you have the hard disk, take the system unit to the dealer for installation if you're nervous about installing it yourself. But if you can't resist a low price for a hard disk drive from a mail-order house (or if a friend gives you one), either you'll have to find a computer service company that will install it for you or you'll have to install it yourself.

Installing the drive isn't especially difficult if you have some experience with hand tools and if the directions that come with the drive are both clear and accurate. You'll probably need only one or two screwdrivers that match the screws used to attach the disk drive to the computer's case—usually a medium-size straight-slot and a #2 Phillips screwdriver. But the instructions that come with do-it-yourself drives probably won't include much detail because a drive can be put into so many different computers, and a mistake can be costly; the drive most likely isn't guaranteed against damage during installation, and poking around inside your computer probably voids its warranty too.

Unless you've successfully installed a hard disk drive before, you're better off paying a professional to do it.

PART II

Preparing Your Hard Disk

Preparing a hard disk for use means more than merely formatting it as you would a diskette. In many cases, this preparation is done for you by the dealer or by the computer-support person at your company. If you bought the computer from a dealer and have discovered that the hard disk isn't prepared, you should be able to take it back to the store and have someone there do it.

If you bought your computer by mail order, however, or if going back to the store isn't convenient, you can use this part of this quick reference to learn whether you need to prepare the hard disk, as well as how to install DOS on it.

FINDING OUT IF YOUR HARD DISK IS READY TO USE

Often the dealer not only prepares the hard disk but—if you bought a copy of DOS at the same time—also installs DOS so that the system is ready to run. To check how much preparation was done on your system, try to start the system from the hard disk by opening the latch on drive A (the left or upper diskette drive) and turning the system on.

You know that DOS is installed and ready to run if you see one of the following:

■ The system prompt (for example, C:\>).

■ A large graphics or text-based window with the words *Start Programs* at the top. (This is the opening screen of the version 4 DOS Shell.)

- A similar window, but with the words *MS-DOS Shell* at the top. (This is the opening screen of the version 5 DOS Shell.)

- The opening screen of an application program. If your computer has been set up for you, it's possible (though not likely with a general-purpose computer) that the person who set up the system also gave DOS the instruction to run a particular program whenever you start or restart the computer.

If your startup ends with any of the displays described, you can be sure that the hard disk has been prepared and DOS has been installed. Go ahead and skip to Part III.

If the system doesn't start as described, you have some work to do; how much depends on the version of DOS you use. If you have version 4 or 5, DOS comes with an installation program that takes care of almost everything for you. It not only puts the DOS files on the hard disk but, if need be, prepares and formats the disk beforehand so that DOS can use it. If you are using an earlier version of DOS, you install DOS in a three-step procedure that involves preparing the hard disk, formatting it, and copying DOS to it.

The following sections describe the basic hard disk setup procedures for these different versions of DOS. Before involving yourself in details, however, take a moment to become familiar with the way DOS treats your hard disk.

Hard Disks and Partitions

Part I described how DOS physically organizes a hard disk by defining tracks and sectors on it. Before DOS can do this, however, you (or someone else) must also provide some logical guidelines by defining one or more *partitions* on it. Partitioning a disk identifies it for DOS in two main ways: It tells DOS whether you want to divide the disk into more than one functional unit, and it tells DOS whether you want the hard disk to be the system's startup disk.

DOS recognizes two types of partition, a *primary DOS partition* and, beginning with version 3.3, an optional *extended DOS partition*. The primary DOS partition is the system disk; DOS starts from it. If you're using DOS version 3.3 or earlier, this partition can be no larger than 32 MB. If you're using DOS version 4 or 5, the primary DOS partition can be much larger, up to 2 GB (2048 MB).

The extended partition, designed to enable DOS version 3.3 to work with hard disks larger than 32 MB, is the remainder of the hard disk. You can create an extended partition with DOS versions 3.3 and later. It can be any size, although if it holds more than 32 MB and you're not using DOS version 4 or 5, you must tell DOS to treat the extended partition as more than one disk drive, each of which holds up to 32 MB.

To partition a hard disk, you use the Fdisk program that comes with DOS. If you have version 4 or 5, the DOS installation program automatically calls Fdisk for you if it determines that your hard disk needs partitioning, so you'll seldom, if ever, need to use Fdisk again. If you do—for example, to install another operating system in addition to DOS or to divide an extended DOS partition into several independent "disk drives"—be sure to back up your hard disk and consult the appropriate documentation beforehand. Tinkering with partitions after you've begun using a hard disk can result in the loss of all information stored on it.

SETTING UP THE HARD DISK WITH VERSION 5 OF DOS

If you're using version 5 of DOS, you have the easiest job of all in terms of preparing a new hard disk and installing DOS. Your installation program comes in a file named Setup on the diskette labeled *Disk 1*. You must use this program to install DOS, so even if you're an experienced user and have installed earlier versions by copying DOS to the hard disk, do it the DOS way this time around. The DOS files are shipped in a special condensed format, and you need Setup to convert them to usable form.

To begin installation, place *Disk 1* in drive A and start or restart your computer. From this point on, Setup does whatever is needed to set up a basic working system on the disk

you specify. If it needs to partition your hard disk, it calls
on the Fdisk program. If it needs to format the hard disk, it
calls on the DOS Format command. Along the way, it tells
you what it's doing and, occasionally, asks you to insert a
diskette or press a key. Setup is easy to use, uses a good
deal of (program) intelligence, and prompts you through
the entire installation. If you are apprehensive or want to
know more about the procedure, consult the documentation
that came with your version of DOS. If you want more information during the installation, press the F1 key to request a display of help information.

When you're finished, skip ahead to Part III.

SETTING UP THE HARD DISK WITH VERSION 4 OF DOS

If you are preparing a new hard disk and installing version
4 of DOS, the installation program you use is activated by
the Select command, which is on the diskette labeled *Install*. Essentially, all you do is place this diskette in drive
A, start or restart your computer, and press the Enter key to
begin. From that point on, the program asks you questions
about your system, helps you partition and format the hard
disk if necessary, and tells you which of the DOS diskettes
it needs at any particular stage of the installation.

Because the Select program does ask you some questions,
it's wise to know the answers before you start. To make the
procedure as easy as possible, find out:

- At least roughly how much memory your computer has,
  and whether it has an added expanded memory board.

- The make and model of printer you'll use and, if it's not
  an IBM printer, whether it's serial or parallel.

- The port to which the printer is connected—for example,
  LPT1 for a parallel printer or COM1 for a serial printer.

Once you have this information, installation should pro-
ceed smoothly if you follow the instructions that appear on
your screen. If, at any point, you want more information,
press the F1 key; Select will display a help message for you.

When you're finished, skip ahead to Part III.

SETTING UP THE HARD DISK WITH VERSIONS EARLIER THAN 4.0

If your version of DOS is 3.3 or earlier, you must do the following to set up your hard disk and install DOS on it:

1. Identify the hard disk to DOS with the Fdisk command.

2. Format the hard disk with the Format command.

3. Install DOS by copying the DOS system files from the system diskettes to the hard disk with the Copy command.

Identifying the Hard Disk to DOS—Fdisk

The procedure that follows shows you how to prepare your hard disk so that DOS can be started from it and only DOS can use it; the procedure applies to IBM PC/XT, PC/AT, and PS/2 computers and compatible models. The instructions make some assumptions about your hard disk and how you want to define it; see the documentation for DOS and your computer if any of the following conditions apply:

■ You have a computer other than the kinds mentioned in the preceding paragraph.

■ You want to run both DOS and another operating system from your hard disk.

■ You don't want to make the primary partition as large as possible.

■ Your hard disk is larger than 60 MB or you want to tell DOS to treat the extended partition as if it were more than one drive.

The following steps include instructions for creating an extended partition if your hard disk can hold more than 32 MB. You can do this only with versions of DOS beginning with 3.3; earlier versions do not allow more than a single DOS partition.

Using Fdisk

Fdisk helps you either set up your hard disk for the first time or change the way DOS uses the hard disk. It's called a menu-driven program because it displays a series of screens from which you choose options much as you choose items from a restaurant menu. Each option you choose causes Fdisk to display another menu, and so the procedure continues until you finish preparing your hard disk.

The Fdisk command has no parameters. If you're using a version of DOS earlier than 3.3, your screen will differ slightly from the following descriptions, but the procedure will be substantially the same except for defining the extended DOS partition.

To use Fdisk to identify your hard disk to DOS, follow these steps:

1. Put the DOS system diskette in drive A and turn the system on or restart it by pressing Ctrl-Alt-Del (hold down the keys marked Ctrl and Alt, and press the key marked Del). DOS might prompt you for the correct date and time as follows:

```
Current date is Tue 1-01-1980
Enter new date (mm-dd-yy): _
```

If you don't see this prompt, skip to step 4.

2. If DOS displays the correct date, simply press the Enter key. Otherwise, type today's date in numeric form, using the date format DOS displays in its *Enter new date* request. (In the United States, for example, you would enter October 16, 1991, as *10-16-91*.) Press Enter after you type the date. DOS prompts you for the time as follows:

```
Current time is 0:01:30.00
Enter new time: _
```

The current time DOS displays will differ, depending on how long your system has been on.

3. If DOS displays the correct time, simply press Enter. Otherwise, type the current time, using a 24-hour clock format. (For example, enter 2:30 P.M. as *14:30*.) Press Enter after you enter the time. Now DOS displays its

opening message and the system prompt, which tells you
that DOS is ready for you to enter a command:

```
The IBM Personal Computer DOS
Version 3.30 (C)Copyright International ....
           (C)Copyright Microsoft Corp ...
A>_
```

4. Enter the Fdisk command as follows:

```
A>fdisk
```

DOS fills the screen with the first menu for the Fdisk
command, as follows:

```
IBM Personal Computer
Fixed Disk Setup Program Version 3.30
(C)Copyright IBM Corporation 1983,1987

FDISK Options

Current Fixed Disk Drive: 1

Choose one of the following:

     1. Create DOS partition
     2. Change Active Partition
     3. Delete DOS partition
     4. Display Partition Information

Enter Choice: [1]

Press ESC to return to DOS
```

(If you have more than one hard disk on the system,
Fdisk displays a fifth menu option, *Select Next Fixed Disk
Drive*. Disregard it.)

5. Press Enter (this selects item 1). Fdisk displays the following menu:

```
Create DOS Partition

Current Fixed Disk Drive: 1

     1. Create Primary DOS partition
     2. Create Extended DOS partition

Enter choice: [1]

Press ESC to return to FDISK Options
```

6. Press the Enter key to choose option 1. If the hard disk has already been prepared by your dealer or someone else, Fdisk responds *Primary DOS partition already exists* and *Press ESC to return to FDISK Options.* Press Esc once to return to the Fdisk menu, then press Esc again to return to DOS. Go on to the heading ''Formatting the Hard Disk.'' If the hard disk hasn't been prepared, Fdisk responds with the following:

```
Create Primary DOS Partition

Current Fixed Disk Drive: 1

Do you wish to use the maximum size
for a DOS partition and make the DOS
partition active (Y/N).........? [Y]

Press ESC to return to FDISK Options
```

The primary DOS partition is the one DOS starts from; it can hold as much as 32 MB. As mentioned at the beginning of this section, these instructions show how to create a primary partition of the maximum size; press Enter to select Y (yes). DOS responds with the following:

```
System will now restart

Insert DOS diskette in drive A:
Press any key when ready...
```

7. The DOS system diskette is already in drive A, so press a key. DOS restarts and again displays the date prompt. Set the date and time again, as you did in steps 2 and 3, if necessary. If your hard disk holds 32 MB or less, go on to the heading ''Formatting the Hard Disk.''

8. If your hard disk holds more than 32 MB and you're using DOS version 3.3, you must identify the remainder of your disk space to DOS. To do this, enter the Fdisk command again, as follows:

```
A>fdisk
```

Fdisk displays the same screenful of options it did in step 4.

9. Again, press the Enter key to select item 1 (*Create DOS partition*). Fdisk displays the same screenful of options it did in step 5.

10. This time, type *2* to choose *Create Extended DOS partition* and press Enter. Fdisk shows a display like the following:

```
Create Extended DOS Partition

Current Fixed Disk Drive: 1

Partition Status  Type   Start  End Size
  C: 1       A    PRI DOS    0  731  732

Total disk space is  979 cylinders.
Maximum space available for partition
is  531 cylinders.

Enter partition size...........: [ 531]

Press ESC to return to FDISK options.
```

The partition size Fdisk displays is the amount of remaining space on the hard disk. Press Enter to devote all of it to the extended DOS partition. Fdisk responds with the following message:

```
Extended DOS partition created
```

11. Press Esc. Fdisk displays a screen like the following:

```
Create Logical DOS Drive(s)

No logical drives defined

Total partition size is  531 cylinders.

Maximum space available for logical
drive is  531 cylinders.

Enter logical drive size........: [531]

Press ESC to return to FDISK Options
```

Fdisk is asking you how to divide this space into one or more logical drives (*logical* because any drive you define acts exactly like an independent disk drive, even though it's not a physically separate piece of equipment).

Press Enter to assign all remaining disk space (up to 32 MB in version 3.3) to one logical drive, then press Esc twice to end the Fdisk program.

Press any key to restart your system and, if necessary, enter the correct date and time as you did earlier.

FORMATTING THE HARD DISK

Warning: Formatting the hard disk erases any files that may be stored on it, so follow this procedure only if the hard disk has not yet been formatted or if you don't need any of the files stored on it.

1. Enter the Format command:

```
A>format c: /s /v
```

DOS displays the following message before starting to format the disk, giving you a chance to cancel the command (because formatting erases any files on the disk):

```
WARNING, ALL DATA ON NON-REMOVABLE DISK
DRIVE C: WILL BE LOST!
Proceed with format (Y/N)?
```

2. Press Y and then press Enter. The light on the hard disk goes on; DOS displays a constantly changing message telling you the head and cylinder number being formatted as it prepares the hard disk for use. Depending on the size of your hard disk, this can be a lengthy process, so don't be concerned if five or ten minutes pass and formatting is still not complete. When DOS finishes, it responds with the following:

```
Format complete
System transferred

Volume label (11 characters, ENTER for none)?
```

DOS is waiting for you to type an identifying name, or volume label, for the disk. DOS displays the volume label each time you display the directory of the drive; you can change this name at any time with the Label command.

3. Type any name of up to 11 characters and press the Enter key. This completes formatting your primary DOS
   partition. DOS responds by telling you how the disk
   space is allocated and then displays the system prompt.

4. If you devoted your entire hard disk to DOS, go on to
   the heading "Copying the DOS Files to the Hard Disk."
   If your hard disk can hold more than 32 MB, format the
   logical drive (probably drive D) that you assigned to the
   extended DOS partition, this time without transferring
   the DOS system files. For example, type:

```
A>format d: /v
```

Copying the DOS Files to the Hard Disk

With the DOS system diskette still in drive A, create a
directory especially for DOS on drive C:

```
A>md c:\dos
```

Now copy the DOS files from the system diskette in drive
A to your DOS directory. Type the following:

```
A>copy *.* c:\dos
```

DOS displays the names of the files as it copies them.
When all the files have been copied, DOS again displays
the system prompt. Because you formatted the hard disk
with the /S option of the Format command, the file COM-
MAND.COM is now in both the root directory and your
new DOS directory. It needs to be only in the root directory, so delete it from the directory named \DOS by typing
the command:

```
A>erase c:\dos\command.com
```

Remove the DOS system diskette from drive A and store it
in a safe place.

If you're using 3½-inch diskettes, you're done; go on to
the next paragraph. If you're using 5¼-inch diskettes, you
must copy the remaining DOS files. Insert the other DOS
diskette in drive A and repeat the preceding command
(*copy* *.* *c:\dos*).

Finally, you need to tell DOS where to find its command
files whenever you start it from drive C. Do this by

creating a special file named AUTOEXEC.BAT, which
DOS looks for whenever it starts up. Type the following,
entering ^Z by holding down the key labeled Ctrl and
pressing Z. If you make a mistake before pressing Enter at
the end of a line, backspace to the error and correct it. If
you notice an error after you press Enter, press the keys
labeled Ctrl and Break and try again; if you notice an error
after pressing Ctrl and Z, retype the entire command:

```
A>copy con c:\autoexec.bat
path c:\dos
^Z
```

DOS responds *1 File(s) copied.* You're done.

TESTING THE HARD DISK

To be sure the procedures were successful, restart DOS
from the hard disk. Open the door on drive A so that DOS
won't try to start from that drive, then restart DOS by
pressing Ctrl-Alt-Del.

If all went well, the system prompt is C> rather than A>,
showing you that the hard disk is the current drive.

If DOS doesn't restart properly, press Ctrl-Alt-Del again,
being sure to hold both the Ctrl key and the Alt key down
while you press the Del key. If DOS still doesn't restart
properly, put the DOS system diskette back in drive A,
close the latch, and press Ctrl-Alt-Del to restart the system
from the system diskette. Go back to the heading "Identifying the Hard Disk to DOS—Fdisk" and repeat the steps.

A ONE-TIME PROCESS

Unless you decide to change the size of the partitions on
your hard disk or you start using another operating system,
you need to use the Fdisk command only when you first
prepare your hard disk. Upgrading to a new version of DOS
is a much simpler procedure, described under the heading
"Installing a New Version of DOS on Your Hard Disk" in
Part VII, "Maintaining Your Hard Disk."

PART III

Configuring DOS for Your Hard Disk

A hard disk has a greater capacity and operates at a greater speed than a diskette. To make the best use of its capacity and speed, however, you have to tailor DOS to handle more files and to move data more quickly. You do this with a text file named CONFIG.SYS.

The CONFIG.SYS file contains configuration commands— commands that tell DOS what devices are attached to your system and that control how DOS uses your computer's memory. You create CONFIG.SYS with a text editor or with a word processor that lets you store a file with no formatting codes or other special characters. You must put CONFIG.SYS in the root directory of the system disk. Each time DOS starts, it carries out the commands in CONFIG.SYS.

To make the most efficient use of your hard disk, your CONFIG.SYS file should include the Buffers command, which specifies how many disk buffers DOS allocates, and the Files command, which specifies how many files DOS can use at the same time. Depending on how your system is set up, you might also need to include the Lastdrive command, which sets the highest drive letter that DOS can recognize. If there is no file named CONFIG.SYS in the root directory of the system disk, DOS assumes default values for each of these configuration parameters.

In addition, although they are not directly related to managing your hard disk, two devices that you create in memory can help speed up operations by reducing the number of

times DOS must access the disk. These devices, both defined in CONFIG.SYS, are a RAM disk, which simulates
a disk drive in memory, and a disk cache, which keeps re-
cently used information in memory. If your version of DOS
includes either VDISK.SYS or RAMDRIVE.SYS, you can
create a RAM disk. If you have either version 5 of DOS or
Microsoft's release of version 4, you can use the file named
SMARTDRV.SYS to create a disk cache. Both are described later.

MEMORY: A BRIEF ASIDE

Beginning with version 5, DOS includes several commands
that help you conserve your system's main memory (0 KB
to 640 KB) by using extended or expanded memory for
several purposes, among them holding part of DOS itself.

This quick reference is not a guide to memory management, but because DOS shuttles your programs and data
between memory and disk, a brief description of different
types of memory and of version 5 commands related to
hard disk management is in order. If you don't have version
5 of DOS, you can skip to the next section.

An IBM or compatible computer can have several different
types of random access memory, or RAM. The type you're
most familiar with, and the type any program can use, is
called *conventional* memory. Because of the way DOS and
your computer work, your system can have up to 1 MB of
conventional memory, of which the first 640 KB can be
used for loading programs and data. The remainder of conventional memory, between 640 KB and 1 MB, is called
reserved memory because it's set aside for special purposes,
such as hardware control and video.

To increase a computer's memory beyond 1 MB, you add
either *extended* or *expanded* memory to the system.
Although both increase the computer's available RAM,
extended and expanded memory differ dramatically in how
they're accessed and managed.

Extended memory begins where conventional memory ends, so it literally extends the 1 MB boundary of conventional memory. You can add many megabytes of extended memory to a system, but it's usable only if your programs are designed to find and take advantage of it; some are, others are not. To keep applications from trying to use the same part of extended memory at the same time, extended memory is usually managed by a program called an *extended memory manager*. Version 5 of DOS includes an extended memory manager named HIMEM.SYS.

If your computer has extended memory, you can use part of this memory to hold DOS. If your system has at least 350 KB of extended memory and an 80386 or 80486 microprocessor, you can also tell DOS to use upper memory blocks (UMBs), into which it can load device drivers (with the Devicehigh configuration command) and certain programs (with the Loadhigh command). Using memory above the normal 640-KB limit in these ways can help you conserve conventional memory and make your system more efficient. Refer to your version 5 DOS documentation for help in using high memory.

Rather than extending the limits of conventional memory, expanded memory represents a large reservoir that a program can draw on, as if through a pipeline. Expanded memory is parceled out to programs in 16-KB blocks known as *pages* that are swapped in and out of a space in reserved memory known as a *page frame*. The program that handles this memory and makes it available to requesting programs is called an *expanded memory manager*. Version 5 of DOS includes an expanded memory manager named EMM386.EXE, which you can use if you have a computer based on the 80386 microprocessor. You can put a RAM disk, a disk cache, or both in expanded memory to conserve your system's conventional memory space.

USING THE BUFFERS CONFIGURATION COMMAND

A buffer is an area of memory that DOS uses to hold data that's being moved between disks and programs. Up to a certain point, having more buffers lets DOS operate more quickly by speeding the flow of data between disks and memory. The Buffers configuration command specifies how many buffers DOS uses.

The optimum number of buffers depends on several factors. Among them are:

- The types of disk drives you use. Typically, an increase in the number of buffers speeds hard disk operations. The actual number of buffers you specify depends on the size of your hard disk. Practical values are 20 buffers for a hard disk up to 40 MB; 30 for a disk of 40 to 79 MB; 40 for a disk of 80 to 119 MB; and 50 for a disk of 120 MB or more.

- The size of your computer's memory. Each buffer reduces available memory by about 532 bytes, so a large number of buffers might cause some programs to run more slowly because they have less memory to work in. If you have version 5 of DOS and a computer with extended memory, however, you can conserve your main system memory by adding configuration commands that let you load both DOS and your buffers in the first 64 KB of extended memory, in the special area called the HMA (High Memory Area).

- The types of programs you use. Some programs suggest or even require a minimum number of buffers. In general, if you use applications that normally access files sequentially rather than by jumping from one place to another, 10 to 20 buffers, especially with the version 4 and 5 look-ahead option, can increase speed by keeping information in memory and reducing the number of times DOS must go out to disk.

■ The number and levels of subdirectories in your file
structure. If you have many subdirectories organized in
several levels, setting 10 to 25 buffers can significantly
speed disk operations.

Specifying too many buffers, however, can slow the system
because DOS might then be able to read a record from disk
faster than it can search through all the buffers. Finding the
optimum number of buffers might require some experimen-
tation. After changing the number of buffers, use your system for a while, note its performance, and then change the
number of buffers and repeat your observations.

DOS uses one of the following numbers of buffers unless
you specify otherwise with a Buffers command in your
CONFIG.SYS file:

2   If your system has 360-KB drives and less than 128
    KB of memory.

3   If your system includes a diskette drive that can hold
    more than 360 KB—for example, the IBM PC/AT

5   If your system has 128 KB or more of memory (DOS
    version 3.3 or later)

10 If your system has 256 KB or more of memory (DOS
    version 3.3 or later)

15 If your system has 512 KB or more of memory (DOS
    version 3.3 or later)

The Buffers configuration command can have three
parameters:

`buffers=number,look-ahead /X`

number is the number of buffers. Valid numbers are 1
through 99. If you have version 4 of DOS and a system
with expanded memory, you can place buffers in expanded
memory with the /X parameter. In this case, *number* can be
from 1 through 10000.

look-ahead, in versions 4 and 5 only, represents a secondary
cache. If you specify *look-ahead*, whenever DOS reads a
sector it also "looks ahead" at following sectors and reads
them into memory as well. *look-ahead* is thus the number of
buffers for holding sectors you want DOS to read beyond
the sector currently being read. You can specify a value
from 1 through 8. Each look-ahead buffer takes about 512

bytes of memory. If you already use a disk-caching program, such as Smartdrive in version 5 of DOS, you should
ignore this look-ahead feature. Your disk-caching program
should work as well as, or better than, a secondary cache
created with the Buffers command.

/X, in version 4 only, tells DOS to put the buffers in expanded memory.

Buffers Example

Suppose you have a 30-MB hard disk and 640 KB of
memory and you regularly use a database program. This
type of configuration would benefit from 20 buffers, so you
would put the following command in CONFIG.SYS:

```
buffers=20
```

If you have version 5 of DOS and a system with at least 64
KB of extended memory, the following commands would
load the HIMEM.SYS extended memory manager, locate
DOS in the HMA, and set aside 20 buffers in the HMA:

```
device=c:\dos\himem.sys
dos=high
buffers=20
```

NEED TO USE MORE FILES?
THE FILES CONFIGURATION COMMAND

DOS keeps track of file usage in one of two ways, depending on how an application program is designed. One of
these ways, typical of applications written for DOS versions 2.0 and later, relies on a DOS-assigned number called
a *handle* to keep track of each open file and device on the
system. The Files configuration command sets the maximum number of such handle-based files and devices that
DOS can use at the same time.

If you don't specify otherwise, DOS assumes eight available handles, five of which are preassigned for use by DOS.
This number is sufficient for most uses, but some programs—especially database programs—must have more
than eight handles available at one time. The manual that

comes with your program should tell you whether you need to increase this value; some programs even include an installation utility that puts the proper Files configuration command in CONFIG.SYS for you.

The Files configuration command has one parameter, which you use as follows:

`files=number`

number specifies the maximum number of files that DOS can use at the same time. *number* can be from 8 through 255; if you don't specify *number*, DOS assumes 8. Each additional open file above 8 increases the memory used by DOS by 48 bytes.

Files Example

Suppose that a program you use needs as many as 20 files available at the same time; you would put the following command in CONFIG.SYS:

`files=20`

NEED MORE DRIVE LETTERS? THE LASTDRIVE CONFIGURATION COMMAND

Unless you specify otherwise, DOS recognizes drive letters A through E. Five drive letters might seem more than adequate, but it isn't hard to use them up. For example, suppose you have one diskette drive; DOS assumes it's both A and B. Further suppose your hard disk can hold 60 MB, and you've divided it into a 30-MB primary DOS partition and a 30-MB extended DOS partition. Each partition must have a different drive letter. Because it's your system disk, the primary DOS partition is drive C; the extended partition is next in line, so it's drive D. Also suppose you define a RAM disk as drive E. You're out of drive letters.

Now, what if you add another hard disk to your system? Or suppose your system is attached to a network, and you must define drives to use the network directories. You need more drive letters.

The Lastdrive configuration command lets you specify the highest drive letter that DOS recognizes. You can use it to specify a maximum of 26 drives.

The Lastdrive configuration command has one parameter, which you use as follows:

```
lastdrive=letter
```

letter specifies the highest drive letter that DOS recognizes. It can be any letter from A through Z. If *letter* represents fewer than the number of disk drives physically attached to the computer, DOS ignores the Lastdrive command.

Lastdrive Example

To allow 10 drive letters, include the following command in CONFIG.SYS:

```
lastdrive=j
```

USING A RAM DISK

A *RAM disk,* or virtual disk, is an area of memory that you tell DOS to use as if it were another disk drive attached to your computer. You can create files and subdirectories on it, copy files to and from it, and even run the Check Disk (chkdsk) command against it. Because it has no moving parts, a RAM disk is much faster than a real disk drive. Using a RAM disk not only saves time, it also saves wear and tear on your real disk drives.

You don't need any additional hardware to install a RAM disk, only a program that persuades DOS to treat a portion of memory as a disk drive—a disk drive that happens to be very fast. Some versions of DOS include such a program; it's called VDISK.SYS starting with version 3 of the IBM releases and RAMDRIVE.SYS starting with version 3.2 of other releases. (VDISK stands for virtual disk.) Most add-on memory cards also include a RAM-disk program. Even if you don't have a RAM-disk program, you might want to skim this topic simply to see what the advantages of a RAM disk are.

To use a RAM disk, you copy the program and data files you need from a real disk drive to the RAM disk and then copy the data files back to the real disk after you finish with them. Copying the data files back is particularly important because the revised version of a file is stored only in memory when you use a RAM disk, and the contents of memory are lost whenever you turn your computer off or restart DOS.

Although its speed is advantageous, using a RAM disk has a cost: Because the memory used by a RAM disk isn't available to DOS or other programs, your system must have enough memory to run DOS and all your application programs without the memory you assign to the RAM disk.

If your computer is equipped with extended memory, or if it contains an expanded-memory board that increases memory in accordance with the Lotus/Intel/Microsoft Expanded Memory Specification, you can tell DOS to use this additional memory for your RAM disk, leaving the more conventional memory space for programs to use.

Making a RAM Disk Work for You

To take advantage of the speed of the RAM disk, you copy the data files, batch files, and programs you'll be working with to the RAM disk. Be sure to leave enough unused space on the RAM disk to allow for the increased size of files that you edit plus any backup files that your application programs create automatically.

To simplify setting up the RAM disk, you can write a batch file (or batch files) to copy to the RAM disk the files and programs you need. If you consistently use the same setup, put the commands in AUTOEXEC.BAT so that the RAM disk will be ready to use when DOS first displays the system prompt. (For more details about AUTOEXEC.BAT, see the section titled "Tailoring Your Startup Procedure with AUTOEXEC.BAT" later in this part of the book.)

If you use a RAM disk regularly, the following precautions are in order:

- Back up your work frequently to a real disk. If the power fails or you forget you're using a RAM disk and turn off the system, all the work you did using the RAM disk will be lost.

- Leave room for enough directory entries. Using all the directory entries keeps you from storing any more files, exactly as if you had filled the disk. Remember, most word processors and text editors create backup files, so you need up to twice as many directory entries as the number of files you work on. Some application programs also create temporary files, which the programs delete before returning to DOS; each temporary file also requires a directory entry.

- A directory entry requires only 32 bytes, so you can safely specify 64 directory entries. That takes up only 2 KB of the RAM disk and helps you avoid the problem of filling the disk. If you'll be working with many small files or using several different application programs, specify at least 128 directory entries.

Defining a RAM Disk

To define a RAM disk, you put a Device configuration command that names the RAM-disk program (either VDISK.SYS or RAMDRIVE.SYS) in CONFIG.SYS and then restart the system. The command parameters specify the capacity, sector size, and maximum number of directory entries of the RAM disk.

The RAM-disk program assigns the next available drive letter to the RAM disk. For example, if you have two diskette drives (A and B), the RAM disk would be drive C; if you have one diskette drive and a hard disk (drive C), the RAM disk would be drive D.

Note: If you have a non-DOS RAM-disk program, such as SUPERDRV.COM from AST Research, Inc., you might have to assign a drive letter to your RAM disk; other details of the command description that follows might also be different. Check the manual that came with your RAM-disk program for differences.

The Device command to define a RAM disk has the following parameters.

For IBM versions of DOS numbered 3.0 and later, use the following command:

```
device=vdisk.sys size sector directory /E
```

For MS-DOS versions 3.2 and later, use this command:

```
device=ramdrive.sys size sector directory /E /A
```

VDISK.SYS or RAMDRIVE.SYS is the program that simulates the disk drive in memory. If the program isn't in the root directory of the system disk, you must include its drive letter and path name.

size is the size, in kilobytes, of the RAM disk. The minimum is 1 if your program is named VDISK.SYS and 16 if it is named RAMDRIVE.SYS. The maximum size of the RAM disk is 4096 KB (4 MB) in version 5, and it is the total amount of memory available on your computer in earlier versions. If you omit *size* or specify an incorrect value, DOS sets *size* to 64.

sector is the size, in bytes, of each sector on the RAM disk. You can specify 128, 256, or 512 with either VDISK.SYS or RAMDRIVE.SYS; you can also specify 1024 with RAM-DRIVE.SYS. If you omit *sector* or specify an incorrect value, DOS sets *sector* to 512 (128 in Microsoft's version 3 and IBM's versions 3 and 4).

directory is the number of directory entries allowed in the root directory of the RAM disk. You can specify from 2 through 512 with VDISK.SYS; you can specify from 2 through 1024 with RAMDRIVE.SYS (4 through 1024 if you're using DOS version 4). Each directory takes up 32 bytes of the RAM disk. If you omit *directory* or specify an incorrect value, DOS sets *directory* to 64.

/E tells DOS to use extended memory for the RAM disk, leaving the maximum amount of memory available for programs. If you use /E, you cannot use /A.

/A tells DOS to use expanded memory for the RAM disk, leaving the maximum amount of memory available for programs. You can specify /A only with RAMDRIVE.SYS (included with non-IBM releases of DOS); use /X for VDISK.SYS. If you use /A or /X, you cannot use /E.

RAM-Disk Example

Assume that your RAM-disk program is stored in the directory \DOS on drive C. To define a 100-KB RAM disk with 256-byte sectors and room for 75 directory entries, you would include one of the following Device commands in CONFIG.SYS:

```
device=c:\dos\ramdrive.sys 100 256 75
```

or

```
device=c:\dos\vdisk.sys 100 256 75
```

The commands to create a 1-MB RAM disk in extended memory with 512-byte sectors and 112 directory entries would be:

```
device=c:\dos\ramdrive.sys 1024 512 112 /e
```

or:

```
device=c:\dos\vdisk.sys 1024 512 112 /e
```

Note: The Device command that identifies the extended memory manager must precede the Device command that creates the RAM disk in CONFIG.SYS.

Now suppose you wanted to run your word processing program using the RAM disk. First you would put one or more Copy commands in AUTOEXEC.BAT to copy the word processing program to the RAM disk (drive D). Then you could change the current drive to the RAM disk and start the word processor, or you could write a batch file to copy the document file (or files) to be edited to the RAM disk, start the word processor, and then copy the document files back to the real disk after you edited them. You could call such a batch file WP.BAT and put the following commands in it:

```
@echo off
cd \wp
copy %1 d:
d:
word
c:
copy d:%1
erase d:%1
cd \
```

To edit a file named REPORT.DOC using the RAM disk, you would type *wp report.doc*; two Copy commands in the batch file take care of transferring the original file from the hard disk to the RAM disk and storing the changed file safely back on the hard disk.

By including a wildcard character (* or ?) as part of the file name you specify, you could use this same batch file to edit a set of files with similar names or extensions. For example, to work with all the files whose names start with LET and whose extension is DOC, you would type the command as *wp let*.doc*. Notice, however, that this would copy all the files that match the file name *let*.doc* to the RAM disk and then copy them back to the real disk, whether or not you had changed them.

MAKING YOUR HARD DISK LARGER

You can't really make your hard disk larger, of course, but a data-compression program can make the disk seem larger by reducing the amount of disk space required to store a file. Such programs—called *file-compression programs*— reduce the size of a file by using various techniques, such as replacing a series of identical characters with a special (shorter) code. Some file-compression programs work only with particular application programs; SQZ!, for example, works only with Lotus 1-2-3. Other file-compression programs, such as Cubit, work with any application program. Version 5 of DOS, in fact, is stored in compressed format on your DOS diskettes.

Because file-compression programs actually change a file before storing it on disk, the compressed file must be expanded to its original content whenever it is copied from disk to the computer's memory. You can't use a compressed file with any program unless you first expand it. Some compression programs automatically compress and expand files whenever DOS copies them between memory and disk; others require you to compress and expand files with a command before and after you use them. In either case, moving a file to or from a disk takes longer.

Using a file-compression program sacrifices file-access speed to gain disk space; the trade-off can be particularly noticeable with larger files (those that can hold 25 KB or more). Whether the trade-off is worth your while is something you must decide.

Using a Disk Cache

Hard disks are much faster than diskettes, but programs are available that make them work even faster. Two common types rely on either a *disk cache* or an *in-memory index*. Where the file-compression programs trade disk-access time for disk storage space, these speedup programs trade available computer memory for disk-access time.

A cache, like a buffer, is an area of memory used to hold data read from a disk. But a cache is much larger than a typical DOS buffer, and the disk-cache program keeps track of what's in the cache and where it was stored on the disk. When DOS asks for more data from the disk, the cache program checks to see whether the data is already in the cache. If the data is there, the cache program returns the data to DOS almost immediately, avoiding the need to read the data from the disk.

Depending on the size of the cache, the techniques that the disk-cache program uses to fill it, and the types of programs you use, the apparent increase in disk speed can be dramatic. If you have version 4 or 5 of MS-DOS, you can use the SMARTDRV.SYS program to create the cache in extended or expanded memory. If, instead, you create the cache in conventional memory, you must remember that the memory used by the cache isn't available to DOS or other programs. If you use several memory-resident programs, such as SideKick, you might find that you have to give up one or two of them to use the cache program.

Creating a Disk Cache with SMARTDRV.SYS

The SMARTDRV.SYS device driver creates a disk cache in extended memory or, if you want, in expanded memory. As already mentioned, a disk cache can speed operations significantly because DOS can retrieve information directly from memory much faster than it can search for and find the information on disk.

Note: If you use SMARTDRV.SYS with extended or expanded memory, be certain the Device command identifying the memory manager precedes the Device command identifying SMARTDRV.SYS in CONFIG.SYS.

To create a disk cache with SMARTDRV.SYS, the Device command takes the form:

```
device=smartdrv.sys size minsize /A
```

SMARTDRV.SYS is the name of the device driver. If the program is not in the root directory (it probably isn't), precede the filename with a drive and path—for example, *c:\dos\smartdrv.sys* if the file is in your DOS directory.

size is the size of the disk cache in kilobytes. *size* can be any value from 128 to 8192 (8 MB). If you don't specify a size, the cache is set to 256 KB. In creating the cache, SMARTDRV.SYS rounds the size to the nearest multiple of 16. If there is not enough memory for the size you specify, it creates a smaller cache with the memory available.

minsize, in version 5 only, specifies the smallest size the cache can be, again in kilobytes. You don't have to specify *minsize*, but if you don't, another program (such as Microsoft Windows) might reduce the cache to suit its own needs, even if that means reducing *size* to 0.

/A tells SMARTDRV.SYS to create the cache in expanded memory instead of in extended memory. If you specify /A, be sure that the Device command in CONFIG.SYS that identifies the expanded memory manager precedes the Device command that creates the disk cache.

SMARTDRV.SYS Example

The following commands in CONFIG.SYS would identify the version 5 extended memory manager (HIMEM.SYS) to DOS and create a 1024-KB disk cache (minimum size 256 KB) in extended memory:

```
device=c:\dos\himem.sys
device=c:\dos\smartdrv.sys 1024 256
```

Both commands assume the files are in the C:\DOS directory.

Speeding Up File Access with the Fastopen Command

An in-memory index to speed up file access requires only the use of the Fastopen command, added to DOS in version 3.3. Each time DOS needs a file, it must search for the subdirectory that contains the file and then search the directory entries for the file itself. On a hard disk with hundreds or thousands of files, all this searching takes time.

The Fastopen command tells DOS to keep an in-memory index of the locations of subdirectories and files as it uses them; the next time DOS is asked for a file or subdirectory, it checks this index before it searches the disk. If the location of the file or subdirectory is in memory, DOS can go directly to it instead of having to search for it on the disk.

If you tend to use the same files or directories over and over, the Fastopen command can make DOS visibly faster. Like a disk cache, Fastopen requires memory that becomes unavailable for other uses. But because only the locations of the files and directories—not their contents—are kept in memory, the amount of memory used is much smaller than the amount required for a disk cache.

The Fastopen command works only with hard disks; it has the following three parameters:

```
fastopen drive=files /X
```

drive is the drive letter, followed by a colon, of the hard disk whose files and subdirectories you want DOS to track.

files is the number of files and subdirectories whose locations DOS is to keep in memory. *files* must be separated from *drive* by an equal sign. If you don't specify *files*, DOS keeps track of the location of the last 34 files and subdirectories (the last 10 in non-IBM releases of DOS).

/X, in versions 4 and 5 only, tells DOS to keep the locations in expanded memory.

Fastopen Example

If you wanted DOS to keep track of the last 75 files and subdirectories used on drive C, you would type the following command:

```
C:\>fastopen c:=75
```

Note: You can enter the Fastopen command only once during a session with DOS. You cannot, for example, start a session with the command *fastopen c:=25* and later decide that you want DOS to keep track of more files. To change the number of files, you must restart your computer.

If you routinely use the Fastopen command with the same number of files, put the command in AUTOEXEC.BAT. To use this command from CONFIG.SYS, use the Install command and include a line like the following in your configuration file:

```
install=c:\dos\fastopen.exe c:=75
```

TAILORING YOUR STARTUP PROCEDURE WITH AUTOEXEC.BAT

In addition to putting configuration commands in a CONFIG.SYS file, you can tailor your system's operation by specifying a series of commands to be carried out or programs to be run each time you start your system. You put the commands in a file named AUTOEXEC.BAT in the root directory of the system disk. Like CONFIG.SYS,

AUTOEXEC.BAT is a text file; it must be in the root directory of the system disk. Each time DOS starts, it carries out
the commands in AUTOEXEC.BAT.

At a minimum, you'll probably want to include the required commands to set the correct date and time. If your
system doesn't have a built-in clock/calendar, put Date and
Time commands in AUTOEXEC.BAT so that DOS will
prompt you to enter the date and time. If your system does
have a clock/calendar, it probably came with a program that
sets the clock that DOS uses from the clock/calendar; put
the command that runs this program in AUTOEXEC.BAT.
(You needn't bother with this if you're using version 3.3 or
later because those versions automatically set the DOS
clock if your system has a clock/calendar.)

To make the best use of your hard disk, you might want to
put other commands in AUTOEXEC.BAT. For example, if
you use programs such as a data compressor or an auto-
matic backup utility, putting the commands that start these
programs in AUTOEXEC.BAT means you won't have to
type the commands each time you start the system. If you
have version 5 of DOS, you should seriously consider including the Mirror command in AUTOEXEC.BAT. This
command, described in Part V, "Working with Files," and
in Part VI, "Protecting Your Hard Disk," can help you
keep track of deleted files and, more important, record the
status of your hard disk so that it can be reconstructed if
the partition table is damaged or the disk is accidentally
formatted.

You can also use AUTOEXEC.BAT to tailor your system,
help DOS find program files, and help you keep track of
your directories with the Path and Prompt commands, described in Part IV of this quick reference guide. The following, for example, is a simple AUTOEXEC.BAT file that
tells DOS where to find external DOS commands (in the
\DOS directory) and application programs (in the \WORD
and \EXCEL directories), uses the Mirror command to
record the status of the hard disk (mirror c:) and to track
deleted files (/tc), clears the screen, and changes the
prompt to display the name of the current directory:

```
@echo off
path=c:\;c:\dos;c:\word;c:\excel
mirror c: /tc
cls
prompt [$p]
```

PART IV

Working with Directories

In most ways, you treat a hard disk as if it were a large diskette, using the DOS directory commands to create, change, and remove directories, and the DOS file commands to copy, erase, rename, and work with your files in other ways. You can also use the Volume and Label commands with a hard disk. However, you can't use the Diskcopy and Diskcomp commands because they are specifically designed to work only with entire diskettes.

The DOS file system is layered, or *hierarchical;* a directory can contain not only files but also other directories, which are called *subdirectories.* These subdirectories, in turn, can contain either files or more subdirectories, creating a structure of directories within directories. Because a drawing of the resulting file organization would look something like an upside-down tree, it is sometimes referred to as a tree-structured file system.

When DOS formats a disk, it creates a top-level directory called the *root directory,* which it identifies with a single backslash character, \. Thus, for example, the root directory of drive C is identified as C:\.

The root directory can hold only a limited number of entries; depending on the capacity of the disk, the number varies from 112 on a 360-KB diskette to at least 512 on a hard disk. As discussed later, however, it's a good idea not to put a lot of unnecessary files in the root directory of your hard disk; limiting the root directory to needed files (such as AUTOEXEC.BAT and CONFIG.SYS) and major subdirectories (such as DOS) helps you keep track of the hundreds or thousands of files that will eventually be stored on the disk.

Unlike the root directory, a subdirectory can hold any number of files and other directories. A subdirectory is simply a file that holds directory entries; there is no arbitrary limit on the size of a file, so there is no arbitrary limit on how many entries a subdirectory can contain. Thus, any of the files in the root directory can be subdirectories, each of which, in turn, can contain any number of files. Disk capacity is the only limit on the number of subdirectories and files you can create.

Within this potential labyrinth of subdirectories, DOS identifies each file by its path name: the file name itself, preceded by the list of directory names (starting with the root) that leads to the directory containing the file. Each directory name is separated from the others by a backslash, and the path can include any number of directory names up to a maximum of 63 characters, including backslashes. Suppose, for example, the root directory contained a directory named WP, which contained a directory named CLIENTS, which contained a file named 12–10LET.DOC; its path name would be \WP\CLIENTS\12–10LET.DOC.

Because DOS keeps track of files by their path and file names, you can give files in different directories the same name and extension. The following two path names, for example, guide DOS to entirely different files on drive C:

```
C:\WP\CLIENTS\12-10LET.DOC
C:\WP\LEGAL\12-10LET.DOC
```

SETTING UP YOUR DIRECTORIES

Your directory structure should provide a logical framework for your work with the computer. You might organize your directories by program type (word processor, spreadsheet, and so forth), by department (such as Marketing, Engineering, and Administration), by some combination of these, or by any other method that matches the way you use the computer. The structure should feel natural, and you should be able to find a file without searching through several similarly named directories.

The following table shows some root-level subdirectories that you might use to contain your most frequently used programs and batch files. You might choose different directory names, but these are the types of files you probably would want to be readily available yet easily distinguishable. All these directories should be in the path you define with the Path command.

Directory	Contains
\DOS	All DOS files (and nothing but DOS files); this directory makes it easy to find a DOS file or change to a new DOS version.
\BATCH	Batch files you use frequently, plus any other files (not including application programs) the batch files might require.
\PGM	Utility programs, programs that are used by your batch files, and application programs that don't require a separate directory.
\WP	The word processing program you use. Document files would be in subdirectories. The name \WP is used generically; you'd probably give this directory a name that identifies the program (\WORD, for example, if you use Microsoft Word).
\SPREAD	The spreadsheet program you use. Spreadsheet files would be in subdirectories. The name \SPREAD is used generically; you'd probably give this directory a name that identifies the program (\EXCEL, for example, if you use Microsoft Excel).
\DB	The database program you use. Database files would be in subdirectories. The name \DB is used generically; you'd probably give this directory a name that identifies the program (\RBFILES, for example, if you use R:BASE System V).

CREATING AND REMOVING DIRECTORIES

There is no correct number of directories to use for your files. If you have to search through dozens or hundreds of files to find the one you need, you probably have too few directories; if it's hard to remember exactly where you stored a file or if you find yourself frequently typing overlong path names, you probably have too many directories. You're looking for a structure that lets you remember where a particular file is stored and that lets you find the file quickly.

Before you start creating directories, do some planning. Consider the programs you use and how you use the computer. If you were setting up a paper filing system for the same jobs you'll be doing with the computer, how would you label the drawers of the filing cabinet? What major categories would you set up inside the drawers? Sketch the directory structure that best seems to match the work that you do.

You'll find that such planning is valuable. Your directory structure will evolve as you add new programs and tasks or as you find that a directory is getting too crowded and it's time to split it. However, wholesale change in a directory structure that has accumulated several hundred files is tedious. Unless you have the version 4 or version 5 DOS Shell or a similar program that lets you select and move groups of files, you must copy the files to their new directory and then erase them from the old one.

You need only the following two DOS commands to manage your filing system:

- Make Directory (typed *md* or *mkdir*, which creates a subdirectory)

- Remove Directory (typed *rd* or *rmdir*, which deletes an empty subdirectory)

Creating a New Directory— Make Directory

Whenever you want to create a new directory, you use the Make Directory command, which has the form:

md *path*

path is the path name of the directory you want to create. If *path* begins with a backslash (\), the path starts at the root directory; if *path* doesn't begin with a backslash, the path starts at the current directory. There is no limit to the number of levels of subdirectories other than the 63-character maximum length of the path name, but try to keep the structure practical. Remember, you're trying to organize your files, not track them through a maze.

Because the Assign, Join, and Substitute commands can mask the real identity of directories, you shouldn't create new directories when any of those commands are in effect.

Make Directory Examples

The following examples assume that the current directory is C:\.

To create a subdirectory named WP in the directory named \MKT on drive C (the current drive), use the following command:

```
C:\>md \mkt\wp
```

To create a directory named WP on the diskette in drive A, use the following command:

```
C:\>md a:\wp
```

Removing a Directory— Remove Directory

Whenever you want to remove a directory, you use the Remove Directory command, which has the form:

```
rd pathname
```

pathname is the path to the directory you want to remove. The directory must be empty. You cannot remove the current directory or the root directory.

Because the Assign, Join, and Substitute commands can mask the actual subdirectory names, you shouldn't remove a directory when any of these commands are in effect.

Remove Directory Examples

The following examples assume that the current directory is C:\.

To remove the directory \MKT on the disk in the current drive, use the following command:

```
C:\>rd mkt
```

To remove the subdirectory WP from the \MKT directory on the disk in the current drive, use the following command:

```
C:\>rd \mkt\wp
```

To remove the directory \LETTERS on the disk in drive A, use the following command:

```
C:\>rd a:\letters
```

KEEPING TRACK OF WHERE YOU ARE

After you create a directory structure, you'll need to move around from directory to directory, doing work here and there. As files accumulate, so do directories. Soon you could lose track of where you are in the directory structure, especially if you use several different programs and you jump from directory to directory as you work with one file after another.

DOS gives you several commands that can help simplify your work with directories:

- The Change Directory command (typed *cd* or *chdir*), which changes or displays the current directory

- The Prompt command, which lets you tell DOS to display the name of the current directory as part of the system prompt

- The Path command, which tells DOS where to find program files that aren't in the current directory

- The Append command, which tells DOS where to find data files (and, in versions 3.3, 4, and 5, program files) that aren't in the current directory

The last two commands let you use your programs and data files no matter where you are in the directory structure.

Changing and Displaying the Current Directory—Change Directory

When you want to change the current directory or see which directory you're working in, you use the Change Directory command, which has the form:

```
cd drive:pathname
```

drive is the letter (followed by a colon) of the drive containing the directory you want to change to or display. If you omit *drive*, DOS assumes the current drive.

pathname is the path name of the directory that you want to become the current directory. If you omit *pathname*, DOS displays the current directory of *drive*. If you're changing to a subdirectory of the current directory, you can omit the current directory from *pathname*.

If you omit both *drive* and *pathname*, DOS displays the current directory of the disk in the current drive.

Change Directory Examples

The following examples assume that the current directory is C:\MKT.

To display the name of the current directory of the current drive, use the following command:

```
C:\MKT>cd
C:\MKT
```

To change the current directory in the current drive to \MKT\WP, use the following command:

```
C:\MKT>cd wp
```

To change the current directory in the current drive to the root directory (\), use the following command:

```
C:\MKT>cd \
```

(The backslash moves you immediately to the root directory from any directory.)

To change the current directory on the disk in drive A to \LETTERS, use the following command:

```
C:\MKT>cd a:\letters
```

To display the name of the current directory on the disk in drive A, use the following command:

```
C:\MKT>cd a:
A:\LETTERS
```

Using the .. Entry to Move Among Directories

When you use the Dir command to list a directory that contains subdirectories, the subdirectories are identified as <DIR>. For example, Dir might display the following:

```
Volume in drive C is HARD DISK
Volume Serial Number is 8C6F-6F84
Directory of C:\


DOS          <DIR>       10-16-90   12:11p
WORD         <DIR>       10-18-90    8:14a
```

When you list the contents of a subdirectory, the display begins as follows:

```
Volume in drive C is HARD DISK
Volume Serial Number is 8C6F-6F84
Directory of C:\DOS


.            <DIR>       10-16-90   12:11p
..           <DIR>       10-16-90   12:11p
EGA     SYS     4885     01-01-91   12:00p
DISPLAY SYS    15682     01-01-91   12:00p
```

The .. entry in such a directory listing represents the directory, usually called the *parent,* that is immediately above the current directory. You can use .. as a form of shorthand that moves you around quickly in a directory structure. For example, if you're in the directory \MKT\WP\MEMOS, you can:

- Type *cd* .. to change to \MKT\WP.
- Type *cd* ..\.. to change to \MKT.
- Type *cd* ..*letters* to change to \MKT\WP\LETTERS.

Showing the Current Directory in the System Prompt

As you become increasingly adept at navigating a multi-level directory structure, you find that an on-screen pointer to the current directory becomes more and more useful. On many systems, DOS is set up to display the name of the current directory for you. That means you don't have to type a Change Directory command to display the current directory; DOS itself takes on the job.

If your system prompt consists only of the current drive letter followed by a greater-than sign (usually C>), you can use the Prompt command to tailor the prompt to include the current directory. In addition, you can use the Prompt command on any system, at any time you want, to show your choice of several other items of system information, such as the time or date, as well as other words or symbols the computer can display. If you put the Prompt command in the startup file named AUTOEXEC.BAT in the root directory of your system disk, your own special prompt will appear whenever you start or restart your computer.

The Prompt command has the following format:

```
prompt string
```

string is a string that defines the new prompt. It can contain any printable character, plus any number of two-character codes to include certain system values in the prompt. Each code begins with a dollar sign; the following table shows the second character of each code and the system value it represents:

Code	Information displayed
t	The time (in the form *hh:mm:ss.hh*)
d	The date (in the form *mm-dd-yyyy*, preceded by an abbreviation of the day of the week)
p	The current directory of the current drive
v	The DOS version number
n	The current drive
g	A greater-than sign (>)
l	A less-than sign (<)

Code	Information displayed
b	A vertical bar (¦)
q	An equal sign (=)
h	A backspace (which erases the previous character)
e	An Escape character
_	(underscore) Start a new line
$	A dollar sign

If any other character follows the dollar sign, DOS ignores both characters.

The string ng, for example, defines the standard system prompt: $n displays the current drive letter, and $g displays the greater-than sign. Because the prompt can include the Escape character, you can use the Prompt command to control the display when the ANSI.SYS console-control program is being used. (CONFIG.SYS must include the command *device=ansi.sys*.)

If you enter a Prompt command with no parameters, DOS resets the system prompt to the standard version.

Prompt Examples

The following examples assume that the current directory is C:\DOS. Each prompt-definition string ends with a space, which moves the cursor one space beyond the end of the system prompt. (The example of the new prompt that follows each Prompt command shows this space.)

To define the system prompt as the current directory enclosed in brackets, use the following command:

```
C>prompt [$p]
[C:\DOS] _
```

To define the system prompt as the current directory enclosed in brackets, followed by a space, the word *Command*, and a colon, use the following command:

```
C>prompt [$p] Command:
[C:\DOS] Command: _
```

To define the system prompt as the date, time, and current directory, each on a separate line, use the following command:

```
C>prompt $d$_$t$_$p
Wed 10-16-1991
16:07:31.56
C:\DOS _
```

To define the system prompt as the time, followed by six
backspaces (to erase the hundredths of a second and seconds), a space, and the current directory enclosed in
brackets, use the following command:

```
C>prompt $t$h$h$h$h$h$h [$p]
16:07 [C:\DOS] _
```

Viewing Your Directories

Once you've created and begun using a directory structure,
it's good to be able to see it all—to see what you've created, what you no longer need, and, possibly, what you
might need to improve. Once again, you can use DOS to do
this. With versions of DOS later than 2.0, there are the Tree
and Check Disk commands described in Part V, "Working
with Files." With versions 4 and 5 of DOS, there is the
DOS Shell described in Part VIII, "Using the DOS Shell."
With version 5 of DOS, there are also the /A and /O parameters of the Directory command. These two parameters
are described here. If you don't have version 5 of DOS,
skip to the heading "Telling DOS Where to Find Command Files—Path."

Beginning with version 5, DOS enables you to view directories and files by attribute (/A) and by sort order (/O).
Although DOS treats directories other than the root as if
they were files, it also records their status as directories,
and the /A and /O parameters of the Directory command
use this status to help you sort directory listings by type or
by grouping directories and files separately. When used in
this way, the Directory command in version 5 has the following parameters:

```
dir /A:D /O:G
```

/A:D causes DOS to display only the names of directories.
The display includes all subdirectories of the current
directory.

/O:G causes DOS to display the names of both directories and files, grouping directories separately at the beginning of the list. Typing this parameter as *lo:-g* causes DOS to list directories at the end rather than at the beginning.

If you have a preference for a particular type of directory listing, version 5 of DOS also includes a variable named *dircmd* that you can use with the Set command to change the normal directory display to the one you want. You can include a Set command (shown as part of the following examples) in the startup file named AUTOEXEC.BAT to tailor your directory display whenever you start or restart your system.

Directory Examples

If the current directory is the root directory of drive C, the following Directory command lists only the subdirectories of the root directory:

```
C:\>dir /a:d
```

If the current directory is \MKT, and it contains the subdirectories \WP and \SPREAD, the following command lists only the subdirectories of \MKT:

```
C:\MKT>dir /a:d
```

To group all subdirectories of the root directory on drive C, listing them ahead of any files in the root directory, you would type:

```
C:\>dir /o:g
```

To group the same subdirectories at the end of the listing, the command would be:

```
C:\>dir /o:-g
```

Finally, to change the normal directory display to a wide listing (*dir /w*) with subdirectories shown first (*dir /o:g*), you could place the following command in AUTOEXEC.BAT:

```
set dircmd=/w /o:g
```

To override these settings, you would use the Directory command from the system prompt and precede the option with a hyphen (for example, *dir /-w* to override the wide directory format).

Telling DOS Where to Find Command Files—Path

The Path command tells DOS where to search for a program file—a file with the extension COM, EXE, or BAT—that isn't in the current directory. By defining a command path, you can use a program or an external DOS command no matter what the current directory is. Because you'll always want DOS to know where you have stored your programs, batch files, and external DOS command files, you should include a Path command in your AUTOEXEC.BAT.

The Path command has the following three parameters:

```
path drive:pathname;
```

drive is the letter (followed by a colon) of the drive containing the disk on which you want DOS to look for command files.

pathname is the path to the directory that DOS should search for command files. You can enter a series of path names separated by semicolons.

If you enter *path* followed only by a semicolon, DOS deletes any command path in effect.

If you enter a Path command with no parameters (simply type *path*), DOS displays the path names it currently searches for command files. If you haven't specified a path, DOS displays *No path*.

Path Examples

To define the command path as the directory named DOS in the root directory of the current drive, use the following command:

```
C:\>path \DOS
```

To define the command path as the directories named
\DOS, \WORD, and \BATCH on drive C, use the following command:

```
C:\>path c:\dos;c:\word;c:\batch
```

Assume that the command path is defined as the directories
in the preceding example. To display the command path,
use the following command:

```
C:\>path
```

DOS responds:

```
PATH=C:\DOS;C:\WORD;C:\BATCH
```

To delete the command path, use the following command:

```
C:\>path ;
```

Telling DOS Where to Find
Data Files—Append

If you're using version 3.3 or later, you can use the Append
command to tell DOS where to look for a data file that isn't
in the current directory. Just as with the Path command,
you can name one or more directories on any disk drive.
The difference between Append and Path is that you normally use the Append command with data files and the
Path command with program files.

The Append command has the following parameters:

```
append drive:path /X:on /X:off /path:on /path:off ;
```

drive is the letter, followed by a colon, of the drive with the
disk that contains the data files (such as A:). If you omit
drive, DOS looks in the directory specified by *path* on the
current drive.

path is the path name of the directory that contains the data
files. You can specify several data paths in one command,
separating them with semicolons.

/X:on makes the data path available to additional DOS
commands; you can specify /X:on (/X in version 3.3) only
the first time you use Append after starting your system.
Specifying /X:on extends the search path by enabling DOS

to find and run programs in appended directories, even if they are not included in a Path command. Specifying /X:off (versions 4 and 5 only) limits searches to the current directory.

/path:on tells DOS to process files for which you include a drive letter, path name, or both as part of a file specification; this is the parameter Append assumes. /path:off tells DOS to ignore file specifications that include a drive or pathname.

If you enter *append* followed by a semicolon, DOS cancels any data path in effect.

If you enter an Append command with no parameters (simply type *append*), DOS displays the path names it currently searches for data files. If you haven't specified a data path, DOS displays *No append*.

Because the Append command can mask the real location of a file, you should use it sparingly. When an application creates a new file, that file is saved in the current directory, not in an appended directory as you might expect.

Append Examples

On starting your system, to tell version 4 or 5 of DOS to search the directory \JIMJ for program files as well as data files:

```
C:\>append c:\jimj /x:on
```

To tell DOS to search for data files in the directories \MKT\WP and \ENG\WP on drive C:

```
C:\>append c:\mkt\wp;c:\eng\wp
```

To display the names of appended directories:

```
C:\>append
```

MOVING VERSION 2 OR 3 OF DOS TO A \DOS DIRECTORY

Note: If you have version 4 or 5 of DOS, or if your DOS files are already in a DOS directory, skip to the topic "Changing the Way DOS Treats Drives and Directories."

Files have a tendency to collect in the root directory, some-times by the hundreds. Finding a computer file under such an arrangement is as difficult as finding a particular paper file among a large number tossed into the same drawer.

When you start off with a new computer and a recent ver-sion of DOS, you're almost certain to install DOS (or find your DOS files already installed) in a DOS directory. Situations differ, however, and with a well-used computer or an older version of DOS (2.1 through 3.3) you might well find that your DOS files are sitting with many others in the root directory on drive C.

The only files that DOS insists be in the root directory are those named COMMAND.COM, CONFIG.SYS, and AUTOEXEC.BAT. Some application programs might also require files in the root directory; the documentation that came with the program should tell you, and the program it-self might create the files when you install it. Reserving the root directory for nothing but files that must be there and subdirectories makes it much easier to use your hard disk. If the DOS files are in the root directory, it's therefore worth the time it takes to move them.

Note: The following procedure assumes that DOS has been installed on your hard disk. If it hasn't—if you still must start the system with the DOS diskette in drive A—turn to the heading "Installing a New Version of DOS on Your Hard Disk" in Part VII and follow the instructions there. After you finish, the DOS files will be in a directory named \DOS.

The following steps show you how to create a directory named \DOS, put the DOS files in it, and remove the DOS files from the root directory. To complete the procedure, you'll need either your original DOS diskettes or working copies of them.

1. Create a directory named DOS in the root directory to contain the DOS files, and then make that directory the current directory by typing the following Make Direc-tory and Change Directory commands:

```
C>md \dos
C>cd \dos
```

2. Put the DOS startup diskette in drive A, and copy the DOS files as follows:

```
C>copy a:*.*
          22 File(s) copied
```

The number of files copied will be different if you're not using version 3.3 of IBM's release of DOS.

3. The file named COMMAND.COM must be in the root directory of the system disk, but you don't also need it in C:\DOS. It's already in the root directory, so delete it from C:\DOS as follows:

```
C>erase command.com
```

If you're using 3½-inch diskettes, skip to step 5.

4. Put the other DOS diskette in drive A, and copy the DOS files it contains as follows:

```
C>copy a:*.*
          31 File(s) copied
```

Again, the number of files copied will be different if you're not using version 3.3 of IBM's release of DOS.

5. So that you'll know which DOS files you can delete from the root directory, print a sorted listing of all the files you copied from the DOS diskettes to C:\DOS by piping the output of the Directory command to the Sort filter command and then redirecting the output to the printer, as follows:

```
C>dir ¦ sort > prn
```

6. Now change the current directory to the root and print a copy of its sorted directory listing, as follows:

```
C>cd \
C>dir ¦ sort > prn
```

7. Take the two printed directory listings and mark all files on the root directory listing that appear on both of the lists.

8. Erase all the files from the root directory that you marked on its directory list.

Now that you have moved the DOS files to a directory named \DOS, you have to do a bit of housekeeping to be sure that DOS knows where to find its files.

Changing CONFIG.SYS

If you have a file named CONFIG.SYS in the root directory of your hard disk, it might contain some Device commands that name certain DOS files.

If it does, you must change these commands so that they refer to the new location of the DOS files (C:\DOS), not to the root directory (C:\).

Verify that the root directory is the current directory and then check CONFIG.SYS by displaying its contents with a Type command, as follows:

```
C>type c:\config.sys
```

If DOS responds *File not found*, CONFIG.SYS doesn't exist, so skip to the heading ''Adding \DOS to the Command Path.''

If DOS displays the contents of the file, check each line to see whether it is a Device command that names a file, such as *device=c:\vdisk.sys*. If it is, use your text editor or word processor (if it lets you store a file with no formatting commands) to change each Device command so that it refers to \DOS, not to the root directory. For example, you would change the file named earlier in this paragraph to *device= c:\dos\vdisk.sys*.

Adding \DOS to the Command Path

Now you use the Path command to tell DOS where to find its command files. You'll put this command in the file named AUTOEXEC.BAT.

First check the contents of AUTOEXEC.BAT with the Type command, as follows:

```
C>type c:\autoexec.bat
```

If DOS responds *File not found*, verify that the current directory is the root and enter the following to create the file containing the Path command you need (press Ctrl-Z where you see ^Z):

```
C>copy con autoexec.bat
path c:\dos
^Z
    1 File(s) copied
C>_
```

If, in response to *type autoexec.bat*, DOS displays a series of commands, edit the file by using a text editor or word processor. If there is no Path command, add the line *path c:\dos* to the file. If there is a Path command (such as *path c:* or *path c:\;c:\word*), add a semicolon and *c:\dos* to the end of the command and save the revised version of your AUTOEXEC.BAT file.

Testing the New DOS Directory

Double-check your work by typing *dir c:\command* to be sure the root directory contains COMMAND.COM, because DOS won't start from the hard disk without it. If it isn't there, put the DOS startup diskette in drive A and copy COMMAND.COM to the root directory.

Next, type *dir c:\dos* to be sure that \DOS contains the DOS files. If you're not sure you can recognize the DOS files, look for files named CHKDSK.COM, FOR-MAT.COM, FIND.EXE, or other familiar DOS command names. If the DOS files aren't there, copy them from the DOS diskettes to \DOS (steps 2 through 4 of the moving procedure).

Now it's time to check to be sure your new setup works. Open the latch on drive A and press Ctrl-Alt-Del to restart the system. DOS should start exactly as it did before. If it doesn't, the problem is most likely one of the following:

■ If DOS displays the message *Bad or missing COM-MAND.COM* and doesn't display the system prompt, then COMMAND.COM isn't in the root directory. Place your startup diskette in drive A, close the latch if necessary (so that DOS will start from drive A) and press Ctrl-Alt-Del again. When DOS is running, copy

COMMAND.COM from the DOS diskette to the root directory on the hard disk, and restart the system.

■ If the system displays a message such as *Bad or missing VDISK.SYS* but DOS does display the system prompt or the prompt for the date and time, a Device command in CONFIG.SYS probably still refers to the root directory instead of to C:\DOS. Go back to the heading "Changing CONFIG.SYS" and follow the instructions there.

When DOS displays the system prompt, check the command path by entering a Path command with no parameters, as follows:

`C>path`

The command path that DOS displays should include C:\DOS (for example, *PATH=C:\DOS* or *PATH=C:\; C:\WORD;C:\DOS*). If DOS responds *No path* or the path doesn't include C:\DOS, go back and repeat the instructions beginning with "Adding \DOS to the Command Path."

If the root directory of your hard disk still contains application programs and data files, you should eventually move them to other directories. As you learn what the files are for, and as you become more comfortable with the tree-structured filing system, you can create directories for them, copy them to the new directories, and delete them from the root directory.

CHANGING THE WAY DOS TREATS DRIVES AND DIRECTORIES

Warning: The Join and Substitute commands let you change the way DOS interprets drive letters. These commands restrict your use of other DOS commands, such as Backup, Restore, and Print, that deal with disks and files. Use these commands sparingly, and check the descriptions of the other disk and file commands in your DOS manual to make certain you understand the restrictions. The Join and Substitute commands cannot be used on a network.

Treating a Disk Drive As If It Were a Directory—Join

The Join command lets you treat a disk in one drive as if it were a directory on a second drive. DOS treats the entire directory structure of the disk in the joined drive as if it were contained in the directory of the disk in the drive to which it is joined. If you use an application program that stores data files only on the program disk, the Join command lets you get around the restriction and store your data files on another disk. Similarly, if you store data files on a diskette and want an application to treat that diskette as if it were a directory on your hard disk, you can use the Join command to do so.

After you join a drive to a directory on another drive, you can't use its drive letter in any DOS command. Because the Join command masks the actual type of disk drive from DOS, you shouldn't use the Backup, Diskcopy, or Restore command when a join is in effect, nor should you enter an Assign or Substitute command that involves a joined drive. If you want to use one of these commands or you need to use the drive, delete the join with the /D parameter. You cannot use the Join command with a network drive.

The Join command has the following three parameters:

```
join drive1: drive2:\directory /D
```

drive1: is the drive that you want to join to a directory on the second drive. The complete directory structure of the drive is joined, beginning at the root, regardless of the current directory.

drive2:*directory* is the drive and directory to which you want *drive1*: joined. *directory* must include the entire path, starting from the root directory of *drive2*. If *directory* doesn't exist, the Join command creates it; if *directory* does exist, it must not contain any files. You cannot join to the root directory of *drive2*.

/D disconnects any join involving *drive1*.

If you enter a Join command with no parameters (simply type *join*), DOS displays all joins in effect.

Join Examples

Suppose you keep certain document files on diskette rather than on your hard disk. Perhaps you carry them from one computer to another. With the diskette in drive A, you can tell DOS to treat the diskette as if it were the directory \DOCS on drive C by typing:

```
C:\>join a: c:\docs
```

If the directory \DOCS doesn't exist on drive C, DOS creates it. If it does exist and isn't empty, DOS displays *Directory not empty*, followed by the directory name.

Assume that you joined drive A to C:\DRIVEA and drive B to C:\DRIVEB. To display the joins in effect, enter a Join command with no parameters, as follows:

```
C:\>join
```

DOS displays the joins in effect:

```
A: => C:\DRIVEA
B: => C:\DRIVEB
```

If no joins are in effect, DOS doesn't display a message.

To delete any joins affecting drive B (such as in the first example), use the following command:

```
C:\>join b: /d
```

Treating a Directory As If It Were a Disk Drive—Substitute

The opposite of the Join command, the Substitute command tells DOS to treat a directory as if it were a disk drive on your system. This lets you store application programs and data files in directories even if the application program doesn't permit the use of path names. If your directory structure has several levels, you can also use the Substitute command to save keystrokes by replacing a long path name with a drive letter.

If you substitute a drive letter for a directory and you then want to substitute the same drive letter for a different directory, you must first delete the original substitution.

Because the Substitute command masks the actual type of disk drive from DOS, you shouldn't use the Assign, Backup, CheckDisk, Diskcomp, Diskcopy, Fdisk, Format, Join, Label, Recover, Restore, or System commands when a substitution is in effect. Because the Substitute command can mask the true directory structure, you should avoid using the Change Directory, Make Directory, Remove Directory, and Path commands when a substitution is in effect. If you want to use one of these commands, delete the substitution. You can't use the Substitute command with a network drive.

The Substitute command has the following three parameters:

```
subst drive: pathname /D
```

drive is the letter, followed by a colon, of the drive you want substituted for *pathname*. *drive* cannot be the current drive. If you specify *drive*, you must also specify *pathname*.

pathname is the path to the subdirectory you want substituted for *drive*; it must begin at the root directory (start with \). If you include a drive letter in *pathname*, it must be different from *drive*. You must specify at least a backslash to name the root directory.

/D deletes a substitution, returning the drive letter to its original meaning.

If you enter the Substitute command with no parameters (simply type *subst*), DOS displays all substitutions currently in effect.

Substitute Examples

Suppose you're using a program that doesn't allow path names when you name a file, but does let you specify a different drive; you want to keep the program in a directory named \MYPROG and its files in a directory named \MYPROG\DOCS, all on the hard disk in drive C. The following Substitute command tells DOS to treat the directory C:\MYPROG\DOCS as if it were drive E:

```
C:\>subst e: \myprog\docs
```

If you want to use several directories for different types of files, enter a Substitute command for each directory, using a different drive letter for each. If you need drive letters beyond E, put a Lastdrive configuration command in CONFIG.SYS to tell DOS the highest drive letter that you will use.

Suppose your spreadsheet program is in C:\SPREAD and the spreadsheets are in subdirectories of that directory. Budgets are in C:\SPREAD\BUDGETS, and budget forecasts are in C:\SPREAD\BUDGETS\FORECAST. If you have to type that path name more than once, you could make your life easier by telling DOS to treat that directory as if it were drive F, as follows:

```
C:\>subst f: \spread\budgets\forecast
```

Note: If you're familiar with batch files or the version 5 Doskey program, which helps you record commands as keyboard macros, you can reduce the typing chores in this example to a single letter. Save the Substitute command as F.BAT, for example, or create a macro named F that carries out the command for you. Then, whenever you want to make this substitution, typing the single letter F will carry out the command.

Suppose you made the substitutions in the first two examples. The following command displays any substitutions in effect:

```
C:\>subst
E: => C:\MYPROG\DOCS
F: => C:\SPREAD\BUDGETS\FORECAST
```

The following command deletes the substitution created by the first example:

```
C:\>subst e: /d
```

PART V

Working with Files

The sheer number of files on a hard disk means you'll probably spend much less time swapping diskettes but possibly more time finding the files you need, clearing out unused files, moving files around, copying files to other disks, and generally keeping house.

This part of the quick reference focuses on some techniques and commands that can help you manage your filing system, showing you how to accomplish the following tasks:

- Name your files to keep track of them better.

- Protect your files against inadvertent change.

- Track deleted files so you can recover some or all of them if you make a mistake.

- Keep your directory listings uncluttered (and keep personal files out of direct view) by hiding selected files and directories.

- Combine files and copy to and from devices by using the Copy command.

- Copy entire directory structures by using the Xcopy and Replace commands.

- Copy only changed files or only those that have changed since a certain date by using the Xcopy command.

- Replace only files that already exist on the target disk or directory—or add only those that don't exist there—by using the Replace command.

- Display and print the directory structure—with or without the names of all the files—by using the Tree and Check Disk commands.

■ Use two batch files—described at the end of this part—to move a file from one directory to another or to find a file anywhere on the disk.

NAMING YOUR FILES

Consistency in naming your files lets you manage them more easily. For example, if you use the extension LET for all files that contain letters, you can type *dir *.let* to display the names of all such files.

Suppose you use the following convention to name files that contain letters:

■ The first three characters identify the recipient.

■ The next two characters identify the month (01 through 12).

■ The next two characters identify the day of the month (01 through 31).

■ The extension is always LET.

TJW1112.LET, then, would be the name of a letter to someone whose initials are TJW, written (or last changed) on November 12. Using this convention, you would start the month or day with a zero if the number is less than 10 so that the parts of the file name always begin at the same position. A letter to TJW written on March 8, for example, would be stored in TJW0308.LET.

This scheme lets you display the names of all files that contain letters by typing *dir *.let*, display the names of all letters written to TJW by typing *dir tjw**, or display the names of all letters written in July by typing *dir ???07**.

With version 5 of DOS, you can also use this scheme with the /O parameter of the Directory command to sort your directory listings alphabetically by recipient, categorically by extension, or chronologically by date. The /O parameter accepts the following characters to determine the type of sort you want: N to sort by name, E to sort by extension, S to sort by file size, and D to sort by date and time. For

example, typing *dir *.let /o:n* would sort all letters alphabetically by recipient, and typing *dir *.let /o:d* would sort
all letters chronologically by date.

Special Extensions

The following table describes some extensions that have
special meaning to DOS. These extensions either are created by DOS or cause DOS to assume that the file contains
a particular type of program or data. Avoid giving your
files any of these extensions.

Extension	Meaning to DOS
BAK	Short for *Backup*. Contains an earlier version of a text file. Edlin (a DOS text editor), word processors, and other programs automatically make a backup copy of a file and give it this extension.
BAS	Short for *Basic*. Contains a program written in the Basic programming language. You can't run this program by typing its name; you can run it only while using the Basic language.
BAT	Short for *Batch*. Identifies a text file that you can create, containing a set of DOS commands that are run when you type the name of the file.
COM	Short for *Command*. Identifies a command file that contains a program DOS runs when you type the file name.
CPI	Short for *Code Page Information*. Describes the characters that a device can use. Used beginning with DOS version 3.3.
EXE	Short for *Executable*. Like COM, identifies a command file that contains a program DOS runs when you type the file name.
HLP	Short for *Help*. Identifies a file containing online help information. The MS-DOS Editor, QBasic, and other programs use this extension.
INI	Short for *Initialization*. Describes how a program should start operating. Used by Microsoft Windows, Microsoft Word, and other programs.
PIF	Short for *Program Information File*. Describes how an application program works. Used by Microsoft Windows.
SYS	Short for *System*. Identifies a file that can be used only by DOS.

Some application programs also use special extensions. For example, Microsoft Word uses DOC to identify a document, BAK to identify a backup version of a document, GLY to identify a file that contains "boilerplate" text, and STY to identify a file that contains a style sheet of formatting specifications. You should avoid using any extensions that have special meaning to your application program; these extensions are usually listed in the program's manuals.

PREVENTING ACCIDENTAL CHANGES AND DELETIONS

If you're using version 3 or later of DOS, you can make a file read-only by using the Attribute command; after you do this, the file can't be changed or deleted until the read-only attribute is turned off. If you don't use Attribute, one inadvertent change or deletion could make you wish you had protected your files this way.

When used to control the read-only status of a file, the Attribute command has the following four parameters:

```
attrib +R -R filename /S
```

+R tells DOS to make *filename* read-only—that is, to deny all attempts to change or erase *filename*.

-R tells DOS to let *filename* be changed or erased.

filename is the name of the file whose read-only status you want to affect. If you enter the command by using *filename* only, DOS displays the name of the file and, if the file is read-only, displays an *R* to the left of the file name. You can check or change the read-only status of a set of files with similar names or extensions by using wildcard characters.

/S applies the Attribute command not only to the file or files specified by *filename* in the specified directory, but also to all matching files in all subdirectories contained in the specified directory. You can specify /S only if you're using 3.3 or a later version of DOS.

It doesn't take long to protect those files that you change infrequently or not at all or those that simply mustn't be changed accidentally. For example, if all the DOS files are in the directory named \DOS on drive C, you can make them all read-only by entering the following:

```
C:\>attrib +r \dos\*.*
```

To make the file CONTRACT.DOC in the current directory read-only, you would enter the following:

```
C:\>attrib +r contract.doc
```

To allow CONTRACT.DOC to be changed, you would enter the following:

```
C:\>attrib -r contract.doc
```

Note: If you're using 3.2 or a later version of DOS, you can also use the Attribute command to control a file's archive attribute, which is used by the Backup and Xcopy commands and by non-DOS backup programs to determine whether a file has been changed since it was last backed up. This use of the Attribute command is described in Part VI under the heading "Controlling the Archive Attribute of a File."

KEEPING YOUR DIRECTORIES UNCLUTTERED

Beginning with version 5 of DOS, the Attribute command gives you another way to manage files and directories: the hidden attribute. Although being able to hide files and directories might seem like a security measure, be aware that it is not—at least not beyond a minimal degree.

What the hidden attribute can do, however, is decrease screen clutter and, to some extent, keep information out of plain sight. When you use the hidden attribute to hide files, DOS doesn't include them in directory listings unless you specifically request entries with this attribute. Thus, you can use the hidden attribute to omit selected files from directory listings and limit screen displays to those items you want to see whenever you use the Directory command.

When used to control the hidden status of a file or a directory, the Attribute command has the same parameters as for the read-only attribute, except that you use +H to hide the entry and -H to make it visible in directory listings. For example, suppose you have a personal file named REVIEW.DOC in a directory named \MYDIR on your hard disk. To hide the directory, you could type:

```
C:\>attrib +h c:\mydir
```

To leave the directory visible but hide the file, you would type:

```
C:\>attrib +h c:\mydir\review.doc
```

To view the file's directory entry, you would use the /A parameter of the Directory command and request hidden files by specifying *a:h*. Thus, the command to see the directory entry for \MYDIR\REVIEW.DOC would be:

```
C:\>dir mydir /a:h
```

TRACKING DELETED FILES

It can happen to anyone. You type *erase* and a file name, press Enter, and the file's gone. If you included wildcard characters, more than one file's gone. But you didn't mean to do that. What now?

This situation happens often enough that file-recovery programs are profitable products in the microcomputer marketplace. If you have version 5 of DOS, however, you don't need extra software. It comes with DOS as a command named Mirror, which works with two other commands named Undelete and Unformat to help you recover lost files. Unformat is described in Part VI, ''Protecting Your Hard Disk.'' Recovering deleted files with Undelete is described here.

The Mirror command records information about files stored on a disk. When you activate a feature called *delete tracking,* Mirror starts a program that stays in your computer's memory and keeps a record of every file you delete from that point on. This record is kept in a hidden file with the system ("for DOS only") attribute. The file is named PCTRACKR.DEL, and it's stored in the root directory of the disk for which you activate delete tracking. If you later find that you need to recover a deleted file on the disk, the Undelete command can use PCTRACKR.DEL to try to recover the information. Because delete tracking is a useful safeguard for your files, you should consider putting the command in AUTOEXEC.BAT so that DOS activates this feature whenever you start or restart your system.

When used to track deleted files, the Mirror command has the following parameters:

```
mirror /Tdrive-entries /U
```

/T*drive* specifies the drive for which you want to start de-lete tracking. The *entries* part of this parameter specifies the number of entries to track. /T*drive* is required; *entries* is optional but, if included, must be separated from /T*drive* by a hyphen. If you don't specify *entries*, Mirror assumes a generous number ranging from 101 to 303 for hard disks of 20 MB and more.

/U causes Mirror to remove the delete-tracking program from memory.

Suppose, for example, that your drive C is a 32-MB hard disk. To start delete tracking for drive C and accept the number of entries Mirror assumes for a disk that size, the command is:

```
C:\>mirror /tc
```

Mirror would then keep a record of every file you delete, up to the 202-entry limit it assumes for a 32-MB hard disk.

To remove delete tracking from memory, you would type:

```
C:\>mirror /u
```

RECOVERING DELETED FILES

With version 5 of DOS, you can recover deleted files with the Undelete command. You can use this command whether or not you've started delete tracking, but recovery is easier and works better with delete tracking in effect. Regardless of the method you use, however, a word of advance warning is in order:

Part I of this quick reference described briefly how DOS stores files in clusters and uses a list called the FAT to keep track of these storage areas. Be aware that Undelete can recover a deleted file only if its directory entry and storage areas have not been reused for another file. Once DOS writes new information over old information, the old information is gone and cannot be recovered. If you need to undelete one or more files, do so as quickly as possible—immediately, if you can. Each time DOS writes information on a disk, your chances of recovering deleted files, especially in their entirety, grow smaller.

The Undelete command has the following parameters:

```
undelete filename /DT /DOS /LIST /ALL
```

filename is the name of the file you want to undelete. You can include wildcard characters to specify a set of files. Precede *filename* with a drive letter and path if appropriate.

/DT tells Undelete to use the information in the delete-tracking file. Undelete assumes this parameter if a delete-tracking file exists. During recovery, Undelete displays the name of each file, tells you whether it can be fully recovered, and asks what you want to do before going on to the next file that matches *filename*.

/DOS tells Undelete to use directory information recorded by DOS. If you use this parameter, Undelete prompts for the first character of each file name before undeleting the file. Undelete assumes this parameter if a delete-tracking file does not exist.

/LIST tells Undelete to list the files it can recover. Unrecoverable files are marked with a double asterisk (**). This parameter tells you what Undelete can do but does not recover any files at the same time.

/ALL tells Undelete to recover all deleted files it can without stopping to prompt for confirmation. If Undelete uses information recorded by DOS, it replaces the first character of each recovered file name with a character such as #. After recovery, use the Rename command to restore the correct file names.

To see a list of all files with the extension DOC on the current drive that can be recovered:

```
C:\>undelete *.doc /list
```

To recover all deleted files with the extension DOC on the current drive, using delete tracking:

```
C:\>undelete *.doc /dt
```

To recover all deleted files with the extension DOC on the current drive, using directory information recorded by DOS:

```
C:\>undelete *.doc /dos
```

COPYING FILES

Starting with version 3.2, DOS includes three commands you can use to copy files: Copy, which has been a part of DOS since version 1 was released, and the newcomers, Xcopy and Replace, added in version 3.2. Why three commands? Wouldn't one be enough?

Each command has its strengths—functions it performs more quickly than the others or, in some cases, functions the other two don't provide at all. The following descriptions of these three commands for copying files point out these differences.

The Copy Command

The Copy command copies one or more files or the output from a device to another file or to the input to a device. Only the contents of a file are copied; its read-only status and archive status are not.

Although the newer copying commands offer some options that the Copy command lacks, Copy still has an advantage and some capabilities not available with either the Xcopy or the Replace command, as follows:

- The Copy command is built into the portion of DOS that is always in memory; DOS doesn't have to find and load a separate command file to carry out the command.

- Only the Copy command can copy to and from a device.

- Only the Copy command can combine several source files into one target file.

The Copy command has the following parameters:

```
copy source /A /B +source target /A /B /V
```

source is the name of the file or device you want to copy. You can use wildcard characters to copy a set of files with similar names or extensions. You can combine several source files into one target file by separating the source file names with a plus sign (+). If you don't specify *target*, the files are combined into the first source file in the series; otherwise, the files are combined into *target*.

target is the name of the file or device to which you want to copy *source*. If you want to copy *source* to the same directory on the same disk, *target* must be different from *source*. If you omit *target* and specify a source file in a different drive or a different directory, the file is copied to a file with the same name in the current directory. You can specify a drive letter, a path name, a file name, or all three as *target*, with the following results:

Target	Result
Drive letter	The source file is copied to a file with the same name in the current directory of the specified drive.
Path name	The source file is copied to a file with the same name in the specified directory.
File name	The source file is copied to a file with the specified name in the current directory.
All three	The source file is copied to a file with the specified name in the specified directory of the specified drive.

/A treats the preceding file in the Copy command (and all subsequent files until it encounters /B) as an ASCII, or text, file. The Copy command assumes you're copying an ASCII file when you combine files or when you copy a file to or from a device. The effect of /A depends on whether you specify it with *source* or *target*, as follows:

- DOS copies *source* files up to the first Ctrl-Z (end-of-file) character; it does not copy any data that follows the first Ctrl-Z.

- DOS writes a Ctrl-Z character at the end of *target*.

/B treats the preceding file in the Copy command (and all subsequent files until it encounters /A) as a binary file. The effect of /B depends on whether you specify it with *source* or *target*, as follows:

- DOS copies *source* files in their entirety (the file size as recorded in the directory entry).

- DOS does not write a Ctrl-Z (end-of-file) character at the end of *target*.

/V verifies that the file was copied correctly. DOS turns verification on, copies the files, and then turns verification off. This parameter is redundant if the DOS Verify option is on. Verification slows the copy procedure.

Examples of Using Copy to Make Copies of Files

If you wanted to copy all files from the directory named \MKT\WP\LETTERS on the disk in the current drive to the current directory on the disk in drive A, you'd use the following command:

```
C:\>copy \mkt\wp\letters\*.* a:
```

To copy all files named FORECAST, regardless of extension, from the directory named \MKT on the disk in drive A to the current directory on the current drive, giving them the same name, you'd use the following command:

```
C:\BUDGET>copy a:\mkt\forecast.*
```

To copy all the files that have the extension LET from the root directory of drive A to the directory named \WP\LETTERS on the current drive, giving the copies the extension DOC, you'd use the following command:

```
C:\>copy a:\*.let \wp\letters\*.doc
```

Examples of Using Copy to Combine Files

To combine the files named FCST.APR, FCST.MAY, and
FCST.JUN in the current directory into a new file named
FCST.2Q in the current directory, you'd use the following
command:

```
C:\BUDGET>copy fcst.apr+fcst.may+fcst.jun fcst.2q
```

To add the files named FCST.MAY and FCST.JUN to the
file named FCST.APR in the current directory, you'd use
the following command:

```
C:\BUDGET>copy fcst.apr+fcst.may+fcst.jun
```

To combine all the files with the extension DOC in the current directory, in the order in which their directory entries
appear, into the file named TOTAL.DOC in the current
directory, you'd use the following command:

```
C:\MKT\WP>copy *.doc total.doc
```

Note: When you use wildcard characters in this way to
combine source files into an existing target file, the original contents of the target file are lost—replaced by the
contents of the combined source files. Although DOS does
display the message *Content of destination lost before copy*,
this message appears after the fact, when it's too late to
stop the copy procedure. When combining files, verify that
your target file either doesn't exist in the specified directory or doesn't contain information you want to keep. If it
does exist and you want other files added to it, use the plus
sign between the names of the source files and specify the
target file name first.

Examples of Using Copy to Copy to and from a Device

To copy the file REPORT.DOC to the display (CON),
you'd use the following command:

```
C:\MKT\WP>copy report.doc con
```

The file is displayed. Using Copy in this way achieves the
same result as if you had used the Type command (*type c:\
mkt\wp\report.doc*).

To copy from the keyboard (CON, short for console) to a file named REPORT.DOC in the current directory, you'd use the following command:

```
C:\MKT\CLIENTS>copy con report.doc
```

Type the lines you want in the file, pressing Enter to start each new line. To end the copy, press Ctrl-Z to mark the end of the file, and then press Enter. If there is no file named REPORT.DOC, DOS creates it. Be careful, though. If a file named REPORT.DOC already exists in the current directory, DOS replaces it with what you typed; you could lose a valuable file this way, so be sure to choose the file name carefully when you copy from the console (keyboard) to a file.

To copy from the keyboard (CON) to the printer (PRN), use the following command:

```
C:\>copy con prn
```

Type the lines to be printed. To print the lines, press Ctrl-Z to mark the end of the file, and then press Enter.

The Xcopy Command

The Xcopy command, like the Copy command, makes copies of files, but it also lets you do the following:

- Copy faster. When you copy several files, Xcopy is much quicker than Copy. Xcopy copies as many source files as will fit into memory at the same time; Copy copies files one at a time.

- Copy an entire directory structure—all the subdirectories in the source directory, as well as all the files in them. If the corresponding directories don't exist on the target disk or directory, the Xcopy command creates them.

- Copy only files whose archive attribute is on—that is, files that have changed since they were last backed up.

- Copy only files that have changed since a particular date.

You can use the Xcopy command for all other routine copy operations except those specific to the Copy command (copying to and from devices, and combining files).

The Xcopy command has the following parameters:

`xcopy source target /A /M /D:date /E /P /S /V /W`

source is the name of the file you want to copy. You can use wildcard characters to copy a set of files with similar file names or extensions.

target specifies the file or device to which you want to copy *source*. You can include any combination of drive letter, path name, and file name. The effect is the same as that described for the Copy command.

/A copies only those files whose archive attribute is on and leaves the archive attribute of the source file unchanged.

/M copies only those files whose archive attribute is on and then turns off the archive attribute of the source file. This tells DOS (or any other program, such as a backup utility) that the file hasn't changed since it was last backed up, and therefore it doesn't need to be backed up.

/D:*date* copies only files whose date of creation or last change (as displayed by the Directory command) is the same as or later than *date*.

/S applies the Xcopy command to all subdirectories contained in *source*. If you specify *source* as a drive letter or as the root directory of a disk, the Xcopy command copies all the directories and files from *source* to *target*. If you don't specify /S, the command copies only files in the source directory, as the Copy command does.

/E creates subdirectories in *target* that match those in *source*, even if they're empty. /E has no effect if you don't also specify /S.

/P prompts you for confirmation before it copies each file specified in *source*.

/V verifies that the copies in *target* were stored correctly. This parameter can slow the operation of the Xcopy command somewhat, but it is good insurance if you're copying critical data and must be sure it's copied correctly.

/W (for *wait*) prompts you to press a key before the Xcopy command begins. This gives you a chance to put the correct diskette in the drive before starting to copy files.

Xcopy Examples

To copy all the files and subdirectories in the directory named \NEWFILES from the disk in the current drive to the current directory on the disk in drive A, you'd use the following command:

```
C:\>xcopy \newfiles a: /s
```

To copy the entire directory structure, starting with \LET-TERS, on the disk in the current drive—including empty directories—to the current directory on the disk in drive A, you'd use the following command:

```
C:\>xcopy \letters a: /e /s
```

To copy all the files whose archive attribute is on from the directory \WP\LETTERS and all the subdirectories it contains on the disk in the current drive to the disk in drive A, turning off the archive attribute of the source files, you'd use the following command:

```
C:\>xcopy \wp\letters a: /m /s
```

To copy all the files that have changed since April 27, 1991, from the directory \WP\LETTERS and all the subdirectories that contain files on the disk in the current drive to the disk in drive A, prompting for confirmation before each copy, you'd use the following command:

```
C:\>xcopy \wp\letters a: /d:4-27-91 /s /p
```

The Replace Command

The Replace command also makes copies of files. Like the Xcopy command, it lets you copy an entire directory structure, and it uses all of the available memory to speed the copying of several files. It doesn't let you base the copy on the archive attributes of the files or on whether they have changed since a certain date, as the Xcopy command does, but it does let you base the copy on whether a source file also exists on the target, as follows:

■ You can copy only the source files that *do* exist on the target—in other words, replace files.

■ Or you can copy only the source files that *don't* exist on the target—in other words, add files.

You can use the Replace command for all other routine copy operations except those specific to the Copy command (copying to and from devices and combining files).

The Replace command has these parameters:

```
replace source target /A /S /R /P /W /U
```

source is the name of the file to be copied. You can use wildcard characters to copy a set of files with similar file names or extensions.

target specifies the drive and path to which you want to copy *source*. You can include only a drive letter and a path name, not a file name.

/A (for *add*) copies only the files specified in *source* that don't exist in *target*. This parameter lets you add files to *target* without replacing files that already exist. If you don't specify /A, only the files specified in *source* that exist on *target* are copied (replaced). If you specify /A, you cannot specify /S or /U.

/S applies the Replace command to all subdirectories contained in *target*. If you specify *target* as the root directory of a disk, the Replace command copies the specified files from *source* to *target*. If you don't specify /S, the command copies files only to the specified *target* directory, just as the Copy command does. If you specify /S, you can't specify /A.

/R replaces files in *target* even if they are read-only.

/P prompts for confirmation before replacing or adding each file.

/W (for *wait*) prompts you to press a key before the Replace command begins. This gives you an opportunity to put the correct diskette in the drive before starting to replace or add files.

/U replaces only files in the target drive or directory that are older than their counterparts in the source drive or directory. If you specify /U, you can't specify /A.

Replace Examples

To replace all files whose extension is BAT in the directory named \BATCH on the disk in the current drive with the files of the same name in the current directory on the disk in drive A, you'd use the following command:

```
C:\>replace a:*.bat \batch
```

To add all files whose extension is BAT in the current directory on the disk in drive A that do not exist in the directory named \BATCH on the disk in the current drive, you'd use the following command:

```
C:\>replace a:*.bat \batch /a
```

To replace all files whose extension is BAT—even if they are read-only—in every directory of the entire current disk with the files of the same name in the current directory on the disk in drive A, you'd use the following command:

```
C:\>replace a:*.bat \ /r /s
```

Note: When you replace a read-only file, the new copy of the file is also given the read-only attribute.

LISTING ALL THE FILES ON THE DISK—TREE

If you have version 4 or 5 of DOS, you can use the DOS Shell at any time to view the directory structure of a disk. If you have an earlier version, however, or if you want to view your directory structure from the system prompt, the Tree command displays the path of each directory on a disk, followed by a list of the subdirectories contained in the directory. To produce a printed copy of this report, send (redirect) the output of the Tree command to your printer with the > redirection symbol (enter *tree > prn*).

You can also tell the Tree command to display the name of each file in each directory and, again, you can print a copy of the report. On a hard disk with several hundred files, however, this list could be several pages long. That's fine if you really want to see where all your files are stored, but it can be a bit much if all you're interested in is the directory structure.

The Tree command has the following parameters:

```
tree drive:pathname /F /A
```

drive is the letter (followed by a colon) of the drive that contains the disk whose directory structure you want to display.

pathname is the path to the uppermost directory you want Tree to display. This parameter is available only in versions 4 and 5 of DOS; earlier versions display the entire directory structure of *drive*.

/F displays a list of the files in each directory.

/A causes Tree to use only standard ASCII characters in its output. This parameter is useful if your printer can't print the graphics characters Tree normally uses. This parameter is available only in versions 4 and 5.

Tree Examples

Assume that the root directory of the disk in drive C contains four subdirectories: DOS, MKT, MFG, and ENG; \MKT and \ENG, in turn, contain subdirectories named WP and SPREAD. To print this directory structure on a printer that can print graphics characters, you'd use the following command:

```
C:\>tree C:\> prn
```

DOS prints the following:

```
Directory PATH listing for Volume MYDISK
Volume Serial Number is 0C39-16E6
C:.
├───DOS
├───MKT
│   ├───WP
│   └───SPREAD
├───MFG
└───ENG
    ├───WP
    └───SPREAD
```

If your printer cannot print graphics, type the command as *tree c:\ /a > prn.*

If you're using a version of DOS earlier than 4, your tree is more of a list, but you'll still see the same information.

To display the name of each file in each directory, as well as the directory structure, of the disk in the current drive, starting with the current directory (C:\), and to pause after each screenful, use the following command:

```
C:\>tree /f ¦ more
```

The files in the root (or current) directory appear at the beginning of the display. Subdirectories, and the files they contain are listed below.

The Tree command is in versions 2.0 and later of the IBM releases of MS-DOS, and in versions 3.2 and later of other releases. If you don't have the Tree command, you can also use the Check Disk command with the /V parameter to display a similar list of all the directories and files on a disk. To do so you would type *chkdsk /v ¦ more.* The Check Disk command displays the list of directories and files on the disk, followed by its usual report on disk storage use and available memory. You could also print the list by typing *chkdsk /v > prn.*

SOME USEFUL BATCH FILES

Because there are so many files on a hard disk, you find yourself spending a lot more time with housekeeping tasks than you would if you were using only diskettes. You spend time creating new directories, getting rid of directories you don't need anymore, rearranging files, copying files to diskettes, and generally tidying up your file structure so that you can keep track of what you have and so that you can keep your disk from filling up.

Two features you'll find particularly useful are the ability to move files from one directory to another and the ability to find a file in any directory on the disk. If you have version 4 of DOS, you can use the Move command in the DOS

Shell to help you move files around. If you have version 5 of DOS, you can use the Shell's Move command or a mouse to move files, and you can use the /S parameter of the Directory command or the Shell's Search command to find files anywhere on a disk. If you don't have all these capabilities, however, the batch files described here can be of great help too:

■ MOVE.BAT lets you move a file from one directory to another with a single command.

■ FINDFILE.BAT lets you locate a file no matter where it's stored on the disk.

Moving Files from One Directory to Another

In a tree-structured filing system on a hard disk, you often want to move a file from one directory to another. The batch file MOVE.BAT lets you move a file or a set of files with similar names or extensions by using a single command instead of the Copy and Erase commands you would otherwise have to type.

To create the file, use a text editor, such as Edlin, or use your word processor if it lets you store a file with no formatting codes. Type the following commands to create MOVE.BAT; the line numbers are for reference only. Even though lines 5 and 9 are shown on two lines here, type each as a single line.

```
1    @echo off
2    if not exist %1 goto QUIT
3    copy %1 %2
4    cls
5    echo The target directory contains the
     following files.
6    echo Please check for the file(s) you moved.
7    dir %2 /w ¦ more
8    echo.
9    echo If file(s) haven't been moved to
     target directory,
```

```
10    echo press Ctrl-Break to cancel. Otherwise:
11    pause
12    erase %1
13    echo.
14    echo File(s) moved and deleted from source.
15    goto END
16    :QUIT
17    echo File(s) not found
18    :END
```

(If you're familiar with batch files, note that you can speed up MOVE.BAT considerably by removing the comments and pauses.)

Here's how MOVE.BAT works, line by line:

■ Line 1 turns echo off so that DOS doesn't clutter the screen by displaying the commands as it carries them out. If you're not using version 3.3 or later of DOS, don't include the @.

■ Line 2 checks to find out whether the file exists. If the file does not exist, it skips to the label QUIT in line 16.

■ Line 3 copies the file (the first parameter, %1) from the current directory to the target directory (the second parameter, %2).

■ Line 4 clears the screen.

■ Lines 5 and 6 display a message.

■ Line 7 displays a wide listing of the target directory, pausing after each screenful if the directory is large.

■ Line 8 echoes a blank line. With most recent versions of DOS, you can type the line as shown (*echo* followed immediately by a period). If this doesn't work, type *echo*, press the Spacebar, hold down the Alt key and type *255* on the numeric keypad (don't use the numbers at the top of the keyboard), release the Alt key, and press Enter.

■ Lines 9 and 10 display a message that gives you a chance to cancel the batch file before the Erase command deletes the source file.

- Line 11 waits for you to press a key before continuing; if you press Ctrl-Break, DOS asks whether you want to cancel the batch command by displaying the message *Terminate batch job (Y/N)?*

- Line 12 erases the file from its original directory.

- Lines 13 and 14 display a blank line and a message telling you that the move has been completed.

- Line 15 skips to the label END.

- Lines 16 and 17 tell you if the file was not found.

- Line 18 ends the batch file.

You have created a command that has the following two parameters:

```
move source target
```

source is the name of the file you want to move (copy and then delete). If you use wildcard characters in the file name, DOS displays the name of each file it copies. If you don't include a path name, DOS assumes the file or files are in the current directory. If you omit *target*, you must include a path name with *source*, specifying a path other than the current directory, because DOS won't copy a file to itself.

target is the name of the directory to which the *source* files are to be copied. If you omit *target*, the file or files are copied to the current directory.

For example, assume that \WP\DOCS is the current directory. To move the file named REPORT.DOC from the current directory to the directory named \WP\REPORTS, you would enter the following:

```
C:\WP\DOCS>move report.doc \wp\reports
```

or

```
C:\WP\DOCS>move report.doc ..\reports
```

To move all the files in the directory named \WP\DOCS to the current directory, you would enter the following:

```
C:\MYDIR>move \wp\docs\*.*
```

Finding a File Anywhere on the Disk

It isn't hard to forget where you stored a file, especially if your hard disk contains hundreds of files in a couple of dozen directories. If you don't have version 5 of DOS, FINDFILE.BAT simplifies the task of finding a file—at the expense of a little disk space—and usually finds the file fairly quickly.

FINDFILE.BAT takes advantage of the /V option of the Check Disk (chkdsk) command, which displays the name of each file. Instead of displaying this list of files, however, FINDFILE.BAT redirects this list to a file named ALLFILES.DAT in a directory named \BATCH and then searches this file with the Find command for all file names that contain the string you specify.

ALLFILES.DAT isn't an especially large file. Its length depends on how many files are on the disk and how long the path names are; each directory entry averages between 30 and 40 bytes, so (estimating generously) on a 20-MB hard disk with 1000 files, ALLFILES.DAT might be 40,000 bytes long.

Because the Check Disk command can take a minute or two on a large hard disk with many files, FINDFILE.BAT doesn't run the Check Disk command unless you specify *new* as the second parameter or unless ALLFILES.DAT isn't in the directory named \BATCH. Except when you're doing something that requires changing many files, you won't have to tell FINDFILE.BAT to run Check Disk very often, so the search usually takes no more time than it takes DOS to search ALLFILES.DAT.

To create FINDFILE.BAT, use a text editor, such as Edlin, or use your word processor if it lets you store a file with no formatting codes. The following are the commands in FINDFILE.BAT; the line numbers are for reference only. Even though lines 7 through 10 are shown on two lines here, type each as a single line. When you've finished, be sure to save FINDFILE.BAT in a \BATCH directory.

```
1    @echo off
2    cd \batch
3    if not "%1"=="" goto OK
4    :INSTRUCT
5    echo.
6    echo COMMAND                  RESULT
7    echo findfile STRING          Searches for
     file names that
8    echo                          contain STRING.
     STRING must
9    echo                          be entered in
     uppercase.
10   echo findfile STRING new      Forces a Check
     Disk command
11   echo                          before searching.
12   goto END
13   :OK
14   if "%2"=="" goto ONE_PARM
15   if "%2"=="new" goto CHKDSK
16   goto INSTRUCT
17   :ONE_PARM
18   if exist \batch\allfiles.dat goto FIND_IT
19   :CHKDSK
20   echo Executing Check Disk command.
21   chkdsk /v > \batch\allfiles.dat
22   :FIND_IT
23   find "%1" \batch\allfiles.dat
24   :END
```

Note: FINDFILE.BAT assumes that a directory named
\BATCH already exists and that FINDFILE.BAT is in it.

Here's how FINDFILE.BAT works, line by line:

- Line 1 turns echo off. If you're not using version 3.3,
  don't include the @.

- Line 2 changes the current directory to \BATCH (where
  FINDFILE.BAT is stored).

- Line 3 skips the instructions if you specified at least one parameter.

- Line 4 is a label that identifies the beginning of the commands that display instructions for using FINDFILE.BAT.

- Line 5 echoes a blank line. If typing *echo.* doesn't work, type *echo*, press the Spacebar, hold down the Alt key and type *255* on the numeric keypad, release the Alt key, and press Enter.

- Lines 6 through 11 display instructions for using FINDFILE.BAT.

- Line 12 goes to the end of the batch file (where it returns to DOS).

- Line 13 is a label that identifies the beginning of the commands that check what you typed as a second parameter.

- Line 14 skips to the label ONE_PARM if you didn't type a second parameter.

- Line 15 skips to the label CHKDSK if the second parameter you typed is *new*.

- Line 16 skips to the label INSTRUCT if the second parameter you typed isn't *new*.

- Line 17 is a label that identifies the command that checks to find out whether there is a file named ALLFILES.DAT in the directory named \BATCH.

- Line 18 skips to the label FIND_IT if there is a file named ALLFILES.DAT in the directory named \BATCH.

- Line 19 identifies the beginning of the commands that run the Check Disk command.

- Line 20 displays a message telling you that DOS is running the Check Disk command.

- Line 21 is the Check Disk command with the /V parameter; the output of the command is redirected to the file \BATCH\ALLFILES.DAT.

- Line 22 is a label that identifies the Find command.

- Line 23 is the Find command that searches for the string you entered as the first parameter.

- Line 24 is a label that identifies the end of the batch file.

Testing FINDFILE.BAT

You have created a command with the following two parameters:

```
findfile STRING new
```

STRING is the string of characters you want FINDFILE to search for. Because you're searching for a file, *STRING* should be part or all of a path name, a file name, or an extension. Because the output of the Check Disk command is uppercase, you must type the characters to search for in uppercase too.

new tells the batch command to run the Check Disk command, creating a new copy of ALLFILES.DAT, before searching for *STRING*.

If you enter the Findfile batch command with no parameters (simply type *findfile*), it should display the following instructions:

```
COMMAND              RESULT
findfile STRING      Searches for file names that
                     contain STRING. STRING must
                     be entered in uppercase.
findfile STRING new  Forces a Check Disk command
                     before searching.
```

The first time you use it, FINDFILE.BAT runs Check Disk because there is no file named ALLFILES.DAT in the directory named \BATCH. To display the names of all files whose names contain EXE, you would type the following:

```
C:\>findfile EXE
```

FINDFILE.BAT would respond by telling you that it's running Check Disk and then would display the names of the files it found. Because it uses the Find command, its response begins with a line that identifies the file searched (\BATCH\ALLFILES.DAT). The output would begin in the following way:

```
Executing Check Disk command.
--------- \batch\allfiles.dat
        C:\AUTOEXEC.BAT
        C:\DOS\ATTRIB.EXE
        C:\DOS\FIND.EXE
        C:\DOS\JOIN.EXE
        C:\DOS\SHARE.EXE
        C:\DOS\SORT.EXE
        C:\DOS\SUBST.EXE
```

Your list would be different, and probably longer, but it should include these files (although not necessarily in the same order or directory).

Notice that, in addition to the files whose extension is EXE, the sample output also includes AUTOEXEC.BAT because it, too, contains the string EXE.

You could limit the output only to files with the extension EXE by including the period in the string you want to find, as follows:

```
C:\>findfile .EXE
```

This time there would be no message, and the command would take much less time because it wouldn't have to run the Check Disk command. And there would be no AUTO-EXEC.BAT in the list of files. From now on, each search would be this fast until you specified *new* to force another Check Disk command or until you erased ALLFILES.DAT from \BATCH.

Whenever you have added or deleted enough files that you think you need a new list to search, add *new* as a second parameter following the search string.

PART VI

Protecting Your Hard Disk

Because of the number of files a hard disk can hold, protecting it means looking after the integrity of both the disk itself and the information on it.

Making backup copies of the files on your hard disk is the most important way to protect yourself against the loss of valuable files. Even if you never mistakenly erase a file (or a series of files), you can still lose files. Hardware and software failures beyond your control can happen. Take the time to back up your files periodically. It's like wearing a seat belt: the cheapest insurance available.

Beyond this routine housekeeping, you can also take some measures to protect the structure of your hard disk—not the files on it, but the information, invisible to you, that enables DOS to use the disk. Without that information, a hard disk can become unrecognizable to DOS and unusable to you. Although hard disks are extremely reliable, there's an old adage about a stitch in time....

The first part of this section shows you how to use three DOS commands, Backup and Restore (which work together) and Xcopy, to back up files from your hard disk and restore them to the hard disk when you need them. The second part describes ways to use the version 5 Mirror command to save a description of your hard disk so you can restore the disk if necessary.

DEVELOPING A BACKUP PROCEDURE

Note: Even when treated with care, diskettes can still be mislaid or accidentally damaged. Making backup copies of your program diskettes protects you if something goes wrong and you need to reinstall a program on your hard disk. Use the Diskcopy command to duplicate your program diskettes, even before you install the programs on your hard disk. The time it takes to make these copies could be one of your better investments.

Backing up all the files on a hard disk could take a drawerful of diskettes: If your average file were 20,000 bytes long (a little more than 13 double-spaced typed pages), a full 30-MB hard disk would have more than 1500 files, and you would need 26 high-capacity (1.2-MB) diskettes to back them all up. If you were using 360-KB diskettes, you'd need 87 of them.

But you don't have to back up all your files. You needn't back up program files, for example, because you've already got the original DOS and application-program diskettes (plus the backup copies you made). Some data files, such as a spelling dictionary, don't usually change, so it isn't necessary to back them up either.

How often you back up your other data files, such as word processor documents and spreadsheets, depends on how often they change. For example, spreadsheets might change quite often while you are preparing a budget but remain unchanged the rest of the year. The backup procedures you use depend on how you use your computer.

No matter how you back up your files, do it regularly. A system can fail, but if you're diligent about backing up your files, such a failure will be more of an inconvenience than a disaster. You never want to spend hours, days, or even weeks re-creating files that you could have backed up in a few minutes.

USING DOS TO BACK UP FILES

You could back up files from your hard disk to diskettes by using the Copy command, but this is tedious, even if you automate the procedure with a batch file: The Copy command works with only one directory at a time, and it can't determine whether a file has changed since it was last backed up. The temptation is to back up everything, which takes more time and uses more diskettes; the result often is that you postpone backing up.

DOS offers the following three commands, which are much better suited to backing up files from a hard disk:

■ The Backup and Restore commands work together, as their names imply, to let you back up only the files you want. You can use these commands to back up or restore files from many directories with a single command.

■ The Xcopy command—a general-purpose file-copying command—offers much the same capabilities as Backup and Restore.

Warning: Don't use the Backup or Restore command if you have entered an Assign, Join, or Substitute command to alter the way DOS interprets drive letters. Because these commands can mask the type of drive, DOS could damage or delete the files you specify in the commands or other files on the disk. For further information about Join and Substitute, see Part IV, "Working with Directories."

Backing Up with the Backup Command

The Backup command makes a backup copy of files for protection against damage to or other loss of files from the hard disk. Beginning with version 3.0 of the IBM release of DOS and version 3.1 of other releases, you can back up files from any type of source disk (diskette or hard disk) to any type of target disk; previous versions back up files only from a hard disk.

Rather than making an exact copy, as the Copy and Xcopy commands do, the Backup command copies and stores files in a way that helps it (and Restore) keep track of the disk and directory from which each file originally came.

Versions of DOS through 3.2 do this tracking by adding path and file name information to the beginning of each file. Beginning with version 3.3, DOS collects the files it backs up in a single file named BACKUP.*nnn* (*nnn* is the DOS-assigned number of the backup disk); path and file name information are in a file named CONTROL.*nnn*, also on the backup disk.

In all versions of DOS, the Restore command uses the path and file name information to return each file, in its original form, to the disk and directory from which it came. Because backup copies of files are not identical in format to the originals, you must use the Restore command to copy them from the backup disk. Also, because the Backup and Restore commands are not the same in all versions of DOS, you should use the same version for backing up and restoring your files.

Unless you're using version 3.3 or later, you must format the target disk before you back up files to it. And unless you use its /A (Add) option, the Backup command erases any files on the target disk before making the backup copies. It displays a warning message before erasing the files, but to be safe, be sure the backup diskette you use doesn't contain any files you must keep.

If the files you want to back up require more than one diskette, DOS prompts you to insert another diskette; be sure to label these diskettes because the Restore command requires that you restore them in the same order in which you backed them up.

DOS displays the name of each file as it is backed up. If the target disk is a diskette, the backup files are stored in its root directory. If the target disk is a hard disk, the backup files are stored in a directory named \BACKUP.

The Backup command sets the following Errorlevel values:

0   Normal completion.

1   No files were found to back up.

2   Some files were not backed up because there was a file-sharing conflict.

3   The backup process was terminated by the user pressing Ctrl-C.

4   The backup process was terminated by a system error.

You can check this value with the *errorlevel* option of the If batch command and use the result to determine which other commands in a batch file are carried out. For further information on the If command, see Kris Jamsa's *MS-DOS Batch Files: Microsoft Quick Reference* (Microsoft Press, 1991).

Warning: If you back up files from a drive that is affected by an Assign, Substitute, or Join command, restoring the files with the Restore command can damage the directory structure of the disk to which the files are restored.

Although not all of the following options are available in every version of DOS, the Backup command can have up to nine parameters:

```
backup source target /S /M /A /D:date /T:time
/F:size /L:logfile
```

source specifies the file or files you want to back up. You can use wildcard characters to back up a set of files with similar names or extensions. You must specify at least a drive letter, followed by a colon, a path name, or a file name; the following list shows what happens if you specify only one of these elements:

Drive letter	DOS backs up all files in the current directory of the disk in the specified drive.
Path name	DOS backs up all files in the specified directory in the current drive.
File name	DOS backs up the specified file from the current directory.

target is the letter of the drive, followed by a colon, that contains the backup disk.

/S backs up files in all subdirectories contained in the current or specified directory.

/M backs up only files that have changed since they were last backed up.

/A adds the backup files to the backup disk rather than erasing the backup disk before starting the backup.

/D:*date* backs up only files that have changed since the date specified in *date*. Specify *date* as you would if you were using the Date command.

/T:*time* backs up all files that have changed since *time* on *date*. Enter *time* as you would if you were using the Time command. You can specify /T:*time* only in certain versions of DOS.

/F:*size* formats the target disk if it isn't already formatted. This option uses the DOS Format command, so be certain the current command path includes the directory containing FORMAT.COM. If you're using version 3.3 of DOS, you can't use the *size* parameter; DOS will format the target disk to match the capacity of the drive the disk is in. If you're using version 4 or 5, this parameter is not required because DOS automatically formats an unformatted disk for you. You can, however, use /F and *size* to format one or more diskettes to other than the capacity DOS assumes for the diskette drive. Acceptable values for *size* are:

Disk size	*size* value
160-KB single-sided, 5¼-inch	160
180-KB single-sided, 5¼-inch	180
320-KB double-sided, 5¼-inch	320
360-KB double-sided, 5¼-inch	360
720-KB double-sided, 3½-inch	720
1.2-MB double-sided, 5¼-inch	1200 *or* 1.2
1.44-MB double-sided, 3½-inch	1440 *or* 1.44
2.88-MB double-sided, 3½-inch	2880 *or* 2.88

/L:*logfile* creates a log file on the source drive that contains the date and time of the backup, the path name and file name of each file that is backed up, and the number of the diskette on which each file is backed up. If a log file already exists, DOS adds the backup information at the end, creating a history of backups for the source drive. If you don't specify a name for the log file, DOS names it BACKUP.LOG and stores it in the root directory of the source drive. You can specify /L or /L:*logfile* only in certain versions of DOS.

Backup Examples

To back up all files with the extension WKS from the current directory on the disk in the current drive to the disk in drive A, you'd use the following command:

```
C:\BUDGET>backup *.wks a:
```

To back up all files with the extension DOC from the directory named \MKT\WP on the disk in the current drive to the disk in drive A, you'd use the following command:

```
C:\>backup \mkt\wp\*.doc a:
```

To back up all files that have changed since they were last backed up, from the entire disk in the current drive (the root directory and all its subdirectories) to the disk in drive A, use the following command:

```
C:\>backup c:\ a: /s /m
```

To back up all files with the extension DOC from the current directory and all its subdirectories on the disk in the current drive to the disk in drive A, adding them to the backup disk, use the following command:

```
C:\>backup *.doc a: /s /a
```

To back up all files from the current directory and all its subdirectories on the disk in the current drive that were changed on or after October 16, 1991, and have not been archived since then, to the disk in drive A, adding them to the backup disk, you'd use the following command:

```
C:\>backup c: a: /m /a /s /d:10-16-91
```

Restoring Files with the Restore Command

The Restore command copies files that you backed up with the Backup command, moving them from the backup disk to the disk you specify. You can restore files to a different drive (for example, back them up from drive C and restore them to drive D), but because the Backup command stores the full path name with each file, either the same directory structure must exist on the disk to which the files will be restored or you must use the /S option to re-create the original directory structure. If you have a series of backup diskettes, DOS prompts you to enter them, as they are needed, in the same sequence in which they were written by the Backup command.

The Restore command sets the following Errorlevel values:

0   Normal completion.

1   No files were found to restore.

3   The restore process was terminated by the user pressing Ctrl-C.

4   The restore process was terminated by a system error.

You can check this value with the *errorlevel* option of the If batch command and use the result to determine which other commands in a batch file are carried out.

Warning: Restoring files that were backed up when an Assign, Substitute, or Join command was in effect can damage the directory structure of the disk to which the files are restored.

Although not all of the following options are available in every version of DOS, the Restore command can have up to 11 parameters:

```
restore source target /S /P /B:date /A:date /M /N
/E:time /L:time /D
```

source specifies the drive that contains the backup disk from which files are to be restored.

target specifies the file you want to restore. You can use wildcard characters to restore a set of files with similar names or extensions. If you don't specify a path name, files that belong in the current directory are restored. If you don't specify a drive letter, the files are restored to the disk in the current drive.

/S restores files in all subdirectories contained in the specified directory.

/P causes DOS to prompt for confirmation before restoring either a file that has changed since it was backed up or a file that is marked as a hidden or a read-only file. This lets you protect files that you have updated since you backed them up. In versions prior to 3.3, this parameter also helps you avoid replacing the hidden system files (files named IBMBIO.COM and IBMDOS.COM, or IO.SYS and MSDOS.SYS, depending on whose version of DOS you're using) with backup copies from a different version of DOS.

/B:*date* restores only files that were created or changed on or before *date*. Enter *date* as you would if you were using the Date command.

/A:*date* restores only files that were created or changed on or after *date*.

/M restores only files that have changed since they were last backed up.

/N restores only files that don't exist on the target disk.

/E:*time* restores only files that were created or changed at or earlier than *time*. Enter *time* as you would if you were using the Time command.

/L:*time* restores only files that were created or changed at or later than *time*.

/D, in version 5 only, displays the names of backed up files that match those you specified as *target* (for example, all backed up files with the extension .DOC if you specified *.doc* in the Restore command.

Restore Examples

To restore the file named REPORT.DOC from the disk in drive A to its original location in the directory named \MKT\WP on the disk in drive C, you'd use the following command:

```
C:\>restore a: c:\mkt\wp\report.doc
```

To restore all files (the root directory and all subdirectories) from the disk in drive A to the same subdirectories on the disk in the current drive, use the following command:

```
C:\>restore a: c:\ /s
```

To restore all files with the extension WKS from the disk in drive A to the directory named \MKT\SPREAD on the disk in the current drive, prompting for confirmation if the file has changed since it was backed up or if the file is marked read-only, you'd use the following command:

```
C:\>restore a: \mkt\spread\*.wks /p
```

If you have version 5, to see a list of the files on the backup diskette that would be restored in the preceding example, you'd type:

```
C:\>restore a: \mkt\spread\*.wks /d
```

Backing Up and Restoring Files with the Xcopy Command

As described in Part V, the Xcopy command works like the Copy command but does its job much faster and gives you much more selectivity in choosing the files to be copied. Although the Xcopy command wasn't designed specifically for backing up files, this selectivity lets you use the Xcopy command instead of the Backup and Restore commands to back up your hard disk. One advantage to using the Xcopy command is that it stores files in the normal fashion on the backup disk; files backed up by using the Backup command can be copied back to the hard disk only with the Restore command.

The Xcopy command and its parameters are described in Part V.

Xcopy Examples

The following examples correspond to the functions of the earlier Backup and Restore examples.

To back up all files with the extension WKS from the current directory on the disk in the current drive to the disk in drive A, you'd use the following command:

```
C:\BUDGET>xcopy *.wks a:
```

To back up all files with the extension DOC from the directory named \MKT\WP on the disk in the current drive to the disk in drive A, you'd use the following command:

```
C:\>xcopy \mkt\wp\*.doc a:
```

To back up all files that have changed since they were last backed up, from the entire disk in the current drive (the root directory and all its subdirectories) to the disk in drive A, turning off the archive attributes of the files on the source drive, use the following command:

```
C:\>xcopy \ a: /s /m
```

To back up all files with the archive attribute set and with the extension DOC, from the current directory and all its subdirectories on the disk in the current drive to the disk in drive A, leaving the archive attribute of the backed-up files on the source disk unchanged, you'd use the following command:

```
C:\>xcopy *.doc a: /s /a
```

To back up all files from the current directory and all its subdirectories on the disk in the current drive, if the files were changed on or after October 16, 1991, and have not been archived since then, to the disk in drive A, turning off the archive attribute of the backed-up files on the source disk, you'd use the following command:

```
C:\>xcopy c: a: /m /s /d:10-16-91
```

To restore the file named REPORT.DOC from the disk in drive A to the directory \MKT\WP on the disk in drive C, you'd use the following command:

```
C:\>xcopy a:report.doc c:\mkt\wp
```

To restore all files (the root directory and all subdirectories) from the disk in drive A to the disk in drive D, you'd use the following command:

```
C:\>xcopy a:\ d:\ /s
```

To restore all files with the extension WKS from the disk in drive A to the directory named \MKT\SPREAD on the disk in the current drive, prompting for confirmation before each file is copied, you'd use the following command:

```
C:\>xcopy a:*.wks \mkt\spread /p
```

BACKING UP AND RESTORING FILES WITH NON-DOS PROGRAMS

Backup programs are available that copy files much more quickly than do the Backup and Restore commands or the Xcopy command. Some of these programs also compress the files as they back them up (to make the most efficient use of storage space) and expand the files when you restore them to the hard disk.

Like the Backup and Restore commands, these programs use special techniques to copy and restore files. Thus, you usually cannot use the backup files they create as if they were standard DOS files; you must use the backup program to restore the files to the hard disk.

Some of the available programs, such as Fastback Plus, let you choose from several options, all related to backing up a hard disk; others, such as PC Tools Deluxe, package hard disk backup with other utility functions. A hard disk backup program can be worthwhile if you must back up many files, especially if you back them up frequently.

USING A TAPE DRIVE INSTEAD OF DISKETTES

If you back up many files and do so frequently, you might find yourself spending a lot of time backing up simply because of the number of backup diskettes you have to juggle. A solution to this problem is to use a backup tape drive; tape drives commonly hold 60 MB or 120 MB, which should be sufficient for all but the largest hard disks and the most stringent backup requirements.

Most backup tape drives are available as either an internal unit—which fits in the space otherwise occupied by a disk drive—or an external unit, which sits beside the computer. The external units generally cost a bit more because they require a separate case and power supply; your choice depends on whether your system has an empty drive bay and on how much space is available on your desktop.

Other storage devices can be used for backing up your hard disk; some of them work much more quickly than tape drives. Removable-cartridge hard disk drives, for example, offer the convenience of working like any other hard disk; some models have two drives, so you can use one drive as your hard disk and the other as a backup unit. Less common cartridge tape units come with capacities of 120 MB or more and offer greater speed as well as greater capacity.

But most of these systems tend to be more expensive than the common tape drives, and many of them use their own methods of storing data, which means that you can exchange data only with someone who has an identical unit from the same manufacturer. In many cases, it would be cheaper to add a second hard disk drive to your computer and use it to back up files from your primary hard disk.

CONTROLLING THE ARCHIVE ATTRIBUTE OF A FILE

In Part V, under the heading "Preventing Accidental Changes and Deletions," you saw how to use the Attribute command to control the read-only attribute of a file or a group of files. If you're using 3.2 or a later version of DOS, you can also use the Attribute command to control the *archive attribute* of a file.

The archive attribute, like the read-only attribute, is part of the directory entry of a file. It isn't displayed by the Directory command, but you can examine it or change it by using DOS or another program. The Backup and Xcopy commands and some of the non-DOS programs that back up files turn off this attribute. Edlin, Microsoft Word, and most other programs that change a file turn on this attribute.

The archive attribute, therefore, tells DOS—or any other program that checks it—whether a file has changed since the last time it was backed up. The archive attribute is used principally by the Backup command, the Xcopy command, and backup programs, to determine which files they should back up. You can control which files are backed up by turning the archive attribute on or off, but be careful not to prevent DOS from backing up files that should be backed up; you could defeat the purpose of backing up files.

Because of the way in which it is stored in the directory entry, you might sometimes see the archive attribute called the *archive bit*.

Altogether, the Attribute command lets you control the read-only and archive attributes (and, in version 5 of DOS, the hidden and system attributes). It can have the following parameters:

```
attrib +R -R +A -A +H -H +S -S filename /S
```

+R turns on the read-only attribute; -R turns it off.

+A turns on the archive attribute; -A turns it off. You can use these parameters with 3.2 and later versions of DOS.

+H, described in Part V, turns on the hidden attribute; -H turns it off. This is in version 5 only.

+S turns on the system attribute (used primarily by programmers); -S turns it off. This, too, is in version 5 only.

filename is the name of the file whose attributes you want to change or display. You can use wildcard characters to specify a group of files with similar file names or extensions.

/S tells DOS to apply the Attribute command to the files in each subdirectory contained in *filename*. If you specify *filename* as *.* (all files on the disk beginning at the root directory) and include /S, the Attribute command is applied to every file on the disk. You can use the /S parameter beginning with version 3.3 of DOS.

Attribute Examples

If you wanted to turn on the archive attribute of the file named REPORT.DOC in the current directory on the disk in the current drive, you'd use the following command:

```
C:\MKT\WP>attrib +a report.doc
```

To turn off the archive attribute of all the files in the directory named \SPREAD on the disk in the current drive and do the same to all the files in its subdirectories, you'd use the following command:

```
C:\>attrib -a \spread\*.* /s
```

SAFEGUARDING YOUR HARD DISK

As you've just seen, DOS helps you safeguard valuable files by providing the Backup and Restore commands, with which you can copy and store files on another disk for safekeeping. When you're working with your data files, DOS also helps out by requesting confirmation before it carries out an Erase command that would remove all files in a directory. And recent versions of DOS protect you from unintended formats by requiring you to type a drive letter and, if you specify a hard disk, by prompting you to verify the command.

Despite these safeguards, you can still lose information accidentally, so beginning with version 5 DOS provides some security here too.

Saving Disk Information with Mirror

The Mirror command described in Part V can do more than track deleted files. You can also use it to record file-storage information about a diskette or a hard disk, and that information can help you rebuild the disk after an inadvertent format. In addition, you can use the Mirror command to save information, called a *partition table,* that describes the way your hard disk is set up. If you save a copy of the partition table, you can gain access to the hard disk if the original partition table is damaged and DOS is unable to recognize the drive.

Including the /T parameter described in Part V, the Mirror command has these parameters:

```
mirror drive: /1 /Tdrive-entries /PARTN /U
```

drive: is the letter, followed by a colon, of the drive whose file and directory information you want to record. For each drive you specify, Mirror creates a read-only file named MIRROR.FIL in the root directory. You can specify more than one drive by separating the drive letters with a space.

/1 (the numeral 1) tells Mirror to keep only one copy of MIRROR.FIL. If you don't specify /1 and Mirror finds an earlier version of MIRROR.FIL, it renames the old file MIRROR.BAK before creating a new MIRROR.FIL.

/Tdrive-entries tells Mirror to start delete tracking, as described in Part V.

/PARTN tells Mirror to save partition information for a hard disk. Because DOS needs this information to recognize a hard disk but can't access the disk if the partition table is damaged, Mirror saves the partition table on diskette in a file named PARTNSAV.FIL. Before carrying out the command, Mirror prompts you for the letter of a diskette drive. Unless you specify otherwise, it uses drive A.

/U, as already described, removes delete tracking from memory.

The following examples show how to use Mirror to save file-storage information and the partition table and how to safeguard the hard disk in case you ever have to unformat it or reintroduce it to DOS.

To keep a record of disk-storage information for the current hard disk (drive C) and a second hard disk (drive D), the command would be:

```
C:\>mirror c: d:
```

Mirror responds by telling you it *Creates an image of the SYSTEM area*, that the drives you specified are being processed, and (if all goes well) *MIRROR successful*.

Note: Storage on your hard disk changes each time you save or delete a file. To ensure that your MIRROR.FIL is complete and up to date, you can include the Mirror command in your AUTOEXEC.BAT file.

A damaged partition table means that DOS can't find and start from your hard disk. You can, however, use the /PARTN parameter of the Mirror command to save a backup copy of the table. To do this, you would place a formatted diskette in drive A and type:

```
C:\>mirror /partn
```

Mirror responds by telling you that you have started the Disk Partition Table Saver and that it has read the needed information from your hard disk. It then tells you that it will save this information in a file named PARTNSAV.FIL, asks for a formatted diskette, and suggests drive A. If the diskette is already in place, you can press Enter. When the procedure is complete, Mirror responds with the message *Successful*.

Unformatting a Disk

Because of the extent of potential loss in terms of programs and data, recent versions of DOS require deliberate effort on your part to format a hard disk. It's not a step to be taken lightly, and the most experienced computer user feels at least a small twinge after pressing Enter to start the process.

Through version 4, formatting a disk means that any files on it become inaccessible to DOS. In effect, you wipe the disk clean when you format it. Beginning with version 5, however, DOS normally performs a "safe" format—one that can be reversed with the Unformat command.

In restoring a disk, Unformat can work either with the files created by the Mirror command or with the file-storage information recorded on the disk by DOS itself. Of these two options, Mirror is much more likely to be able to restore the disk to its original condition; relying on DOS alone will probably mean the loss of some files. You don't want to chance losing important—possibly critical—files through the inadvertent use of either the Erase command or the Format command, so if you have version 5 of DOS, give serious thought to making Mirror part of your everyday work with DOS.

You can use Unformat with either a diskette or a hard disk, as long as you are not trying to undo a format in which you changed the capacity of a diskette or specified the /U (unconditional) parameter. Specifying /U causes a format like that performed by all versions of DOS prior to 5. An unconditional format cannot be undone.

The complete form of the Unformat command is:

```
unformat drive: /J /L /TEST /PARTN /P /V
```

drive: is the letter, followed by a colon, of the drive containing the disk to be unformatted.

/J checks the disk in *drive* to verify disk-storage information recorded by the Mirror command, but it does not unformat the disk at the same time.

/L produces either of two results, depending on whether you also specify the /PARTN parameter:

- /L without the /PARTN parameter causes Unformat to rebuild the disk and to assume there is no Mirror file to work from. In this case, Unformat searches the disk directly, listing all the files and directories it finds. When this search phase is complete, Unformat prompts for confirmation before actually rebuilding the disk. When the process is complete, subdirectories in the root directory are named SUBDIR.1, SUBDIR.2, SUBDIR.3, and so on. Directories and files below this level, however, retain their original names. For example, a path that was \MKT\WP\REPORT.DOC before an inadvertent format becomes \SUBDIR.1\WP\REPORT.DOC after unformatting with the /L parameter.

- /L with the /PARTN parameter causes Unformat to display the disk's partition table.

/TEST tells Unformat to show how it will rebuild the disk without actually doing so. It does not use files recorded by the Mirror command.

/PARTN, used without the /L parameter, restores the partition table of a hard disk. For this parameter to work, you need the partition-information file recorded on a diskette by the /PARTN parameter of the Mirror command.

/P sends the messages displayed by Unformat to the printer attached to the first parallel port (LPT1).

/U unformats the disk without using the Mirror files; its effect is the same as using /L without the /PARTN parameter.

Note: The following examples are for information only. Do not enter them unless you need to rebuild your hard disk. To prepare for such an emergency, create a DOS startup diskette with the /S parameter of the Format command, copy UNFORMAT.COM and the current CONFIG.SYS file to it, and keep it in a safe place so you can start the system from drive A.

To verify that the files created by the Mirror command agree with the system information on the disk, without actually rebuilding the disk, the command would be:

```
A>unformat c: /j
```

To do the same without using disk-storage information recorded by Mirror, the command would be:

```
A>unformat c: /test
```

To unformat the hard disk, using the Mirror file:

```
A>unformat c:
```

To unformat the hard disk, using information recorded by DOS instead of Mirror:

```
A>unformat c: /l
```

or

```
A>unformat c: /u
```

To rebuild the partition table of the hard disk, using the PARTNSAV.FIL file stored on a diskette in drive A:

```
A>unformat c: /partn
```

To unformat a data diskette in drive A, using the Mirror files:

```
C:\>unformat a:
```

To unformat a data diskette in drive A, using DOS file-storage information:

```
C:\>unformat a: /u
```

PART VII

Maintaining Your Hard Disk

A computer is made up of electrical and mechanical components. Of the two, the mechanical portions, such as the keyboard, printer, and disk drives, are more prone to failure; the electrical portions simply don't have moving parts to wear out. (This isn't to say that you can't have problems with the electrical portions, such as the memory or the display adapter—just that any problems you experience are much more likely to arise from the mechanical elements.)

The hard disk drive has plenty of moving parts. The platters spin constantly; although the read/write heads don't contact the surfaces of the platters (at least under normal circumstances), they are frequently moved back and forth to the spots on the platters where information is to be read or recorded. Considering the amount of movement in a hard disk drive, today's systems are remarkably reliable; it's not unusual for a drive to hum away merrily for several years without a problem.

The high capacity and speed of the hard disk drive are possible because it is sealed in an airtight enclosure, so cleanliness isn't as important to the well-being of your hard disk as is the case with the keyboard or a diskette drive. But you can still help prolong the life of your hard disk drive and reduce the chance of problems. This section describes some steps you can take, most of which have two goals: reducing the amount of head movement and minimizing the effect of physical shock.

Although these measures can reduce the likelihood of hard disk failure, don't be any less diligent about backing up your files and, if you have version 5 of DOS, making a copy of the hard disk's partition table. It's the unpredictability of failure that makes such safeguards so important, regardless of how well you treat your system.

LEAVE THE SYSTEM ON

A computer, like a light bulb or a VCR, experiences extra stress each time you turn it on. You can prolong the life of your computer by turning it on and off as infrequently as possible. Computers don't require much electricity; leaving the system on doesn't cost much and will probably save you money over the life of the system by reducing maintenance costs.

After you turn your system on, don't turn it off until you're through with it for the day. (Don't, however, leave an image displayed on the screen for hours at a time; turn down the brightness control or use a program that blanks the screen or creates changing patterns or images on it.)

There's one exception to this practice. When you start using a brand-new computer, leave it on day and night for the first week or so. If a part is going to fail, chances are it will fail early in its life. You want it to fail as quickly as possible so that you can have it repaired while the machine is still under warranty and, in the case of your hard disk, before you have filled it with valuable files.

KEEP IT CLEAN

Cleanliness is the easiest preventive maintenance you can provide for your computer. You don't have to be a fanatic about it: Personal computers are fairly hardy, so the normal home or office environment is usually just fine. But the mechanical portions of the system will experience less wear if you keep them clean.

Heat is a natural enemy of the machine. Keep the temperature of the room comfortable for you, and don't lay objects on the display or system unit so that you block the ventilating holes. Keep the dust down; you don't want a layer of dust to build up inside the machine because it acts as an insulator and increases the operating temperature.

It isn't necessary to try for an antiseptic environment, but if there's a noticeable amount of dust where you use the computer, you can reduce the chance of a problem by putting a dustcover over the keyboard, display, and system unit when they're turned off. One of those expensive, custom-fitted covers isn't necessary; a piece of plastic or tightly woven nylon will do nicely.

WHAT ABOUT SURGES, SAGS, AND SPIKES?

The electric power from your wall plug isn't perfect. Sometimes the voltage rises a bit: a surge. Sometimes the voltage falls a bit: a sag. Occasionally the voltage might momentarily rise and fall over as little as a few thousandths, or even millionths, of a second: a spike.

Most of these anomalies go unnoticed, but a severe irregularity—a long surge or sag, or a particularly high spike—can cause your computer to reset or your hard disk to behave erratically. If this happens while the computer is reading from or writing to a disk, data on the disk—or even the disk itself—can be damaged.

You can buy a device called a surge suppressor to smooth out the variations in the power, but seek some advice before buying one; some of the cheaper ones don't offer much more than a false sense of security. And you might not need one at all—the power supplies in most IBM and IBM-compatible computers are remarkably tolerant of power fluctuations. If you have used your computer for several months and haven't noticed any erratic behavior, chances are you don't need a surge suppressor. But if there are large industrial users of electricity in your neighborhood, or if a power-hungry device such as an air conditioner is on the same circuit as your computer, or if electrical storms are common in your part of the country, it might be a good idea to get a surge suppressor. Just be sure to get one that does the job.

A surge suppressor won't help, however, if the power goes off. For protection from power outages, you need something that continues to provide electricity itself. Such a device is called an uninterruptible power supply, or UPS. It switches your system to a battery-operated power supply that provides 110 volts when the utility company's power fails and will run your computer for 10 to 20 minutes (depending on the capacity of its battery). A UPS isn't meant to be an alternate source of power; it simply keeps your computer running long enough for you to save files and shut the system down in an orderly fashion. Uninterruptible power supplies are usually rated in volt-amperes (VA); one providing 400 to 600 VA should be adequate for a system including a hard disk and display.

MAKING LIFE EASIER FOR YOUR HARD DISK

A hard disk drive, like any other piece of machinery with moving parts, eventually wears out. Each time the drive reads or writes a file, it must move the read/write head to the proper position above the surface of the platter. By reducing the amount of such head movement you can prolong the life of your hard disk. You can take two steps to cut down on head movement: Take advantage of a program, such as a RAM disk or a disk cache (or both), that uses the computer's memory as a temporary replacement for disk storage, and try to keep your files stored in contiguous sectors. These measures usually have the happy side effect of making file operations noticeably faster.

Substituting Memory for Disk Operations

Disk drives are mechanical, memory is electronic. Memory operations are faster, require less power, and don't cause wear and tear on moving parts. If you have enough available memory, dedicating a portion of it to a RAM disk (described under the heading "Using a RAM Disk" in Part III) lets you transfer some disk operations to memory; but remember to copy all changed files from memory back to the disk drive before you shut down the system. (If you don't, you'll lose whatever changes you made to the files.)

In a similar fashion, a disk-cache program like SMARTDRV.SYS (described under the heading "Making Your Hard Disk Larger" in Part III) substitutes memory operations for disk operations but doesn't require you to explicitly save any files that have changed.

Some disk-cache programs, such as SMARTDRV.SYS and Lightning, write changes to disk as you create or modify files; although this technique might eliminate some of the speed advantage of the cache, it protects you from losing work if the power fails or the system goes down while you're working. Other disk-cache programs don't write changed sectors to the disk until they need the memory where the changed sectors are stored or until you finish working with the file. Although this technique is faster, it exposes you to the possibility of lost work—or even lost files—if a failure occurs. If you're using a disk-cache program that doesn't update the disk whenever you make a change, be sure to save the file often to minimize the likelihood of problems.

If you don't have enough memory for either a RAM disk or a disk-cache program, consider adding more memory or making more memory available (for example, by eliminating some memory-resident programs). You'll find that your system operates more quickly when it works with disk files—which is most of the time—and you'll cut down your disk drive's workload.

Dealing with File Fragmentation

If possible, DOS stores files in adjacent, or contiguous, sectors. As files are deleted and new files are stored, however, files can become fragmented—stored in nonadjacent or, as DOS refers to them, noncontiguous sectors. DOS can still use a file that is fragmented, but the disk drive must do more work: If a file is fragmented into three different groups of nonadjacent sectors, the drive must move the head to each group of sectors to read the entire file.

As more and more files become fragmented, disk operations can be noticeably slowed and the disk drive must move the head more than if the file weren't fragmented. You can restore files to contiguous sectors by backing up the entire hard disk, erasing all the files, and then restoring the files; it sounds time consuming, and it is.

But you don't have to go through all this. Several programs are available that let you pack all the files on a hard disk into contiguous sectors in a single operation. You make one selection from a menu and go do something else for a while—usually no more than 10 to 20 minutes—letting the program do the tedious work. One of the first such programs available is part of a package called the Mace Utilities; others include the Norton Utilities, PC Tools Deluxe, and Disk Optimizer.

The amount of disk fragmentation depends on what types of programs you use, how large your files are, and how often you use your computer. You can check disk fragmentation with one of the disk-optimization programs mentioned in the preceding paragraph; if the program shows a large number of files stored in noncontiguous sectors, pack the files. Doing this periodically reduces head movement and speeds program operation.

WHEN YOU MOVE YOUR COMPUTER

A hard disk contains delicate mechanisms, but is housed in an enclosure that protects it against mild bumps and shocks. You needn't baby the system, but treat it with the same care you would give a stereo or VCR. Don't be afraid to slide it across a desk or carry it from one desk to another, but be careful not to drop it or bang a heavy object into it.

Pay particular attention when you move the system, especially if it will be carried in a truck or car; park the disk-drive heads (more on parking in a moment) and pack the system in its original shipping container, including the foam or Styrofoam cushions usually placed at the corners of the carton. (Also take these precautions if the hard disk drive must be removed from the system unit.)

Parking the heads means moving them to a position over an area of the platter where no data is stored. This way, if the drive should receive a shock that causes the head to bang against the surface of the platter, no recorded data will be damaged. Some drives automatically park the heads each time you turn the system off, but others require that you park the heads by running a program, usually called something like PARK.COM or MOVE.COM.

The documentation that came with your system probably describes any precautions you should take when you move the system, including any specific instructions required to park the heads. As with backing up your hard disk, taking a moment here is cheap insurance against a potentially damaging loss.

INSTALLING A NEW VERSION OF DOS ON YOUR HARD DISK

This section describes the procedure to follow in upgrading with versions of DOS *prior to* 4.0—for example, upgrading from version 3.1 to 3.3. Upgrading to version 4 or 5 of DOS is a much simpler process because these versions come with the installation programs described in Part II under the headings "Setting Up the Hard Disk with Version 5 of DOS" and "Setting Up the Hard Disk with Version 4 of DOS."

If you are upgrading to version 5 of DOS, the installation program guides you through the process with a series of full-screen displays and prompts. Simply place the diskette labeled "Disk 1" in drive A, start or restart your computer, and follow the instructions you see.

Similarly, if you are upgrading to version 4 of DOS, put the DOS disk marked "Install" in drive A, restart the system by pressing Ctrl-Alt-Del, and follow the prompts on the screen. If you want, glance through the version 4 section in Part II ahead of time to familiarize yourself with the installation program and the few items of information DOS asks you to provide.

Upgrading with Other Versions of DOS

If DOS is installed on your hard disk and you want to install a newer version other than version 4 or 5, you must copy two system files that DOS requires as well as the DOS command and data files.

This requires the following two commands:

1. The System command to copy the hidden DOS files
2. The Copy command to copy the DOS command and data files

The system files—IBMBIO.COM and IBMDOS.COM, or IO.SYS and MSDOS.SYS, depending on whose version of DOS you're using—are hidden files, so you don't see them in the output of the Directory command. You can copy them only with the System command. The System command has one parameter, the drive letter of the hard disk to which you want to copy the system files.

Example of Installing a New Version of DOS

Installing DOS on your hard disk requires only a few steps. The following procedure assumes that you have a directory named \DOS on the hard disk for the DOS files. If you keep your DOS files in some other directory, substitute the name of that directory for \dos in steps 3 and 5.

If your DOS files are now in the root directory of the hard disk, create a directory named \DOS by typing *md c:\dos*, and follow the procedure as shown. After you have installed the new version, you'll have to delete the old DOS files from the root directory and update the files named CONFIG.SYS and AUTOEXEC.BAT. (If you need help, refer to the sections "Changing CONFIG.SYS" and "Adding \DOS to the Command Path" in Part IV.

To install a new version of DOS, use the following steps:

1. Put the DOS system diskette (labeled "Startup" or, in versions earlier than 3.3, simply "DOS") in drive A, close the latch, and turn the system on (or, if the system is running, restart it by pressing Ctrl-Alt-Del).

2. When DOS displays the system prompt (A>), type the System command, as follows:

```
A>sys c:
```

DOS copies the two hidden files and responds *System transferred.*

3. Now copy the remaining files on the system disk with the Copy command, as follows:

```
A>copy *.* c:\dos
        22 File(s) copied
```

The number of files copied varies in different versions of DOS.

4. The file COMMAND.COM must be in the root directory of the hard disk, so copy it to the root directory and delete it from \DOS by entering the following:

```
A>copy command.com c:\
        1 File(s) copied
A>erase c:\dos\command.com
```

5. If you're using 3½-inch diskettes, you're done; go on to step 6. Otherwise, take the system diskette out of drive A, put it in a safe place, and put the second DOS diskette (labeled "Operating" or, in versions earlier than 3.3, "Supplemental") in drive A.

Copy these additional DOS files with another Copy command, as follows:

```
A>copy *.* c:\dos
         31 File(s) copied
```

Again, the number of files copied varies with different versions of DOS.

6. That's it. Now open the latch on drive A so that DOS will start from the hard disk, and press Ctrl-Alt-Del. You should see the sign-on message of the new version you just installed. If you don't, go back to step 1 and repeat the procedure.

Part VIII

Using the DOS Shell

Versions 4 and 5 of DOS include the DOS Shell, a graphically oriented program that lets you manage your files and disks by selecting items with the mouse or the keyboard and choosing commands from lists called *menus*. The DOS Shell offers two primary advantages over the DOS command line: It is highly visual, and it cuts down on the need to type commands, file names, and path names. With the Shell, you can even run programs by selecting from a menu and, occasionally, typing a brief response to a prompt.

This part of the quick reference is a brief guide to some of the features of the version 5 Shell that are related to using and managing a hard disk. It is not intended to teach you how to use the DOS Shell. If you are not familiar with the basics of using the DOS Shell, refer to your DOS documentation or, if you have version 5, to the fifth edition of the Microsoft Press book *Running MS-DOS* (1991).

Note: If you have version 4 of DOS, your Shell is similar to the one in version 5, but differs in some significant ways— for example, the names assigned to certain commands. The following descriptions can help you relate your shell conceptually to hard disk management, but for details you should refer to your documentation or to the online Help feature that describes the commands and procedures in your version of the Shell.

WHY USE THE DOS SHELL?

Everything you've already learned about managing directories and files from the system prompt applies when you use the Shell, but the Shell provides some capabilities that DOS doesn't have by itself. First and foremost, the Shell is graphical. That means it uses diagrams, pictures, and menus to make your work easier and more intuitive. For example, the Shell diagrams your directory tree on screen so that you can see the subdirectories you've created and the way they are related to one another. In addition, the Shell lets you:

■ Use either a mouse or special keys on the keyboard to select files, choose commands, change directories, and perform other tasks

■ Display more than one directory if you so choose

■ Create and remove directories and move from one directory to another just as you can from the system prompt, and also rename directories (which you can't do from the system prompt)

■ Control the attributes of your files just as you can from the system prompt

■ Display detailed information about files and directories, including the size of a directory (useful when you want to back up or copy an entire directory)

■ Copy files just as you can from the system prompt, and also copy multiple files or move them from one directory to another with a single command, even if their names don't lend themselves to the use of wildcards

■ Find a file anywhere on your disk with a single command

■ Associate file extensions with programs so that choosing a file with a given extension automatically starts the program associated with it

■ Group your programs in convenient ways and limit access to certain programs by assigning passwords to them

■ Start several programs and switch among them with a feature called the *Task Swapper*

STARTING THE SHELL

If DOS runs the Shell automatically when you start or restart your computer, your startup ends with a screen similar to the one in Figure 8-1. This illustration shows the Shell as it appears on a computer that can display graphics. The Shell looks somewhat different if you display it in text (character) mode. The mouse pointer, for example, is a rectangular block instead of an arrow.

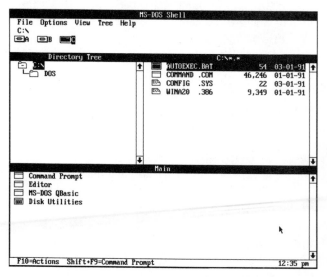

Figure 8-1. *The opening screen of the version 5 DOS Shell.*

If DOS does not run the Shell automatically, you can start the Shell by typing its name: *dosshell.*

Note: To change the display mode used by the Shell, you use the Display command on the Options menu. A dialog box opens to show you a list of display options suited to your video hardware. Select an option either by pressing the Up and Down direction keys or by clicking with the mouse. If you want, tab to or click on Preview at the bottom of the dialog box to see what the screen will look like if you change to the display mode you highlighted.

Getting Help

Both the version 4 and version 5 Shells include online Help that you can access at the press of a key (or the click of a mouse button). In both versions, you press F1 to request help information—for example, about a selected command, menu, or dialog box. Both versions also provide access to an index of Help topics and to help with the keyboard whenever you're viewing Help information. In the version 5 Shell, you also have a Help menu, through which you can request the Help index and keyboard help, as well as information on Shell basics, commands, procedures, even help on using Help.

THE FILE LIST AND THE PROGRAM LIST

When you start the version 5 Shell, the opening screen is normally divided horizontally into two distinct areas, both shown in Figure 8-1. The top portion is called the *File List* area; it is where the Shell displays the directory tree (on the left) and a list of files in the current directory (on the right). The File List area is very important in terms of using the Shell to manage your hard disk.

The lower portion of the Shell window, titled *Main*, is called the *Program List* area; it is where the Shell displays the names of programs you can run. Until you add programs of your own, the Program List area includes at least two choices: Command Prompt, which lets you work at the DOS system prompt, and Disk Utilities, which gives you access through the Shell to the Format, Quick Format, Undelete, Disk Copy, Backup, and Restore commands.

Unless you previously chose an alternative display format (from the View menu), the version 5 Shell starts up with the File List/Program List display described above. During startup, the Shell reads directory and file information for the current drive into memory. If you have a relatively large number of directories and files on the disk, this process can take a short while, so the Shell displays a box with the message *Reading Disk Information* and tells you the number of file and directory entries it has read into memory. When all the information is in memory, the Shell fills in the directory and file names on the screen.

The left side of the File List area, labeled *Directory Tree*, shows a diagram of all the directories in the root directory of the current disk. If your computer doesn't have graphics capability, or if you're running the Shell in text mode, a set of square brackets ([]) appears to the left of each directory. If your computer has graphics capability, or if you're running the Shell in graphics mode, each directory is identified by a small picture of a file folder. The brackets or folders are connected by lines that diagram the directory structure in a display similar to the output of the Tree command. If the directory contains subdirectories, a small plus sign in the brackets or file folder lets you know that the "branch" contains additional directory levels.

The right side of the screen (initially labeled with the letter of the current drive and the identifier *.*) lists all of the files in the root directory.

If you're using the keyboard to operate the Shell, you can use the Tab key to move clockwise through the different areas of the screen. (Press Shift-Tab to move counterclockwise.) If you're using a mouse, you can select any area of the screen, or any item, by moving the mouse pointer to it and clicking the left button.

CREATING, REMOVING, AND RENAMING DIRECTORIES

In the DOS Shell, the equivalent of the Make Directory (md) and Remove Directory (rd) commands are the Create Directory and Delete commands on the File menu that appears when the File List area is selected. This menu also includes a Rename command, which you can use to rename directories—a task that you can't carry out from the DOS system prompt.

Creating a New Directory

To create a directory in the Shell, select the directory in which you want to create the new directory. Use the Tab key to select the directory tree window and the Up and Down direction keys to highlight the directory you want. If you are using a mouse, scroll up or down if necessary, and then simply point to the directory you want and click the left mouse button.

Choose Create Directory from the File menu. The Shell displays a dialog box titled Create Directory. Type the name of the new directory in the text box, and then press Enter or click on OK. The new directory appears in the directory tree.

Removing a Directory

When you delete files and directories at the system prompt, you type *erase* (or *del*) to delete a file and *rd* (or *rmdir*) to delete a directory. The Shell does not have—or need— two separate commands for deleting directories and files. Instead, the Delete command on the File menu handles both files and directories. What the Shell deletes depends on whether you select a file or a directory before choosing the Delete command.

To remove a directory, you must first check that the directory is empty. Select the directory you want to delete and, if it contains any files, delete them before you try to delete the directory. Next choose the Delete command from the File menu. The Shell displays a dialog box titled Delete Directory Confirmation, with the options Yes, No, and Cancel. Choose Yes to carry out the command. The directory disappears from the directory tree.

Renaming a Directory

To rename a directory, you use the same command that you use to rename files—Rename. What the Shell renames depends on whether you select a file or a directory before choosing the Rename command.

To rename a directory, select the directory you want to re-name, and then choose the Rename command from the File menu. The Shell displays a dialog box titled Rename Directory and shows the current name of the directory. Type the new name in the text box, and then press Enter or click on OK. The new name of the directory appears in the directory tree.

MOVING AROUND THE DIRECTORY TREE

With the DOS Shell, you don't need the Prompt command to help you keep track of the current directory, and you don't need the Directory command to show you the contents of a directory. The File List area displays both the name of the current directory and the names of the files in it. The File List area can also help you move up or down the sublevels of your directory tree, it can display the contents of two directories simultaneously, and it lets you decide in what order to display the files in each directory.

Expanding and Collapsing the Directory Tree

The plus sign in the folder or brackets to the left of a directory name tells you that the directory contains other subdirectories and that you can see those directories by pressing the Plus key. You can expand all or part of the directory tree, either to move up or down its various levels or to change the level of detail displayed on screen.

Once a "branch" of the directory tree is expanded, a minus sign appears in its folder (or brackets) to tell you that you can collapse the branch by pressing the Minus key or hyphen if you no longer want to see or use the subdirectories it contains. To expand or collapse a branch with the mouse, simply click on the plus or minus for the appropriate directory.

You can also use the commands on the Tree menu to expand and collapse individual directories or the entire tree.

Changing Directories

To change to a new directory, simply select that directory from the directory tree. If the directory you want isn't displayed, you can scroll through the list with the Up and Down direction keys or the PgUp and PgDn keys. You can also press a letter key to jump to the first directory entry that starts with that letter. (You can do the same with file names.) If you have a mouse, you can use the scroll bar to the right of the directory tree to scroll through the list. When you select a directory, the file list on the right side of the screen changes to display the files in the new directory.

If you want to look at a directory on a different drive, select the appropriate drive letter from those displayed at the top of the screen and, if necessary, choose the specific directory you want to see.

Viewing Two Directories Simultaneously

Sometimes you'll find it useful to display two directories at the same time. For example, you might want to compare the contents of a directory containing letters to clients and a directory containing letters to suppliers. Or you might want to see which files on a diskette are newer than the matching files on your hard disk. The DOS Shell makes this easy to do.

To display two directories simultaneously, choose the Dual File Lists command from the View menu. The screen splits, and you see two directory trees and two file lists, one above the other. To display a particular drive or directory, choose the one you want. You can use any of the Shell commands to work with either directory. To return to a single directory tree, choose Single File List or All Files from the View menu if you don't want the Program List displayed; choose Program/File Lists from the same menu to return to the "normal" Shell display.

Note: Sometimes the file list is not updated to reflect files you've been creating or deleting. If you notice this happening, simply choose Refresh from the View menu to tell the Shell to update the display.

Changing the Order of the File List

When you first start the DOS Shell, the File List displays file names in alphabetic order. You can easily change this order to make it easier to find the files you want. You can also tell the Shell to display only those files having a particular file name or extension.

To change the way the Shell displays the file list, choose the File Display Options command from the Options menu. The Shell displays a dialog box containing several buttons and two additional choices. Select the appropriate button to tell the Shell to display files by name, extension, date, size, or even the order in which they are stored on the disk. If you choose Display Hidden/System Files, the list of file names includes files that are normally hidden from view. If you choose Descending Order, the file names are listed in reverse order (Z to A, latest to earliest, or largest to smallest).

If you want to limit the files shown, type a file name in the Name field. Wildcards are allowed. For example, if you are browsing through word processor documents, you could enter *.ltr in the File Display Options dialog box to show only the letters in each directory you select.

Viewing the Details

As directories and files accumulate on your hard disk, you sometimes want or need more information than a directory listing or a directory tree can display. You might, for example, want to know how large a directory is. At those times, use the All Files command from the View menu or the Show Information command from the Options menu. When you do, the Shell displays a box full of detailed information about the current directory and any files you've selected. Included in the types of information you see are file attributes, directory size and number of files, and disk statistics, including the number of files and directories on it and the amount of storage space remaining.

PREVENTING ACCIDENTAL CHANGES AND DELETIONS

The DOS Shell gives you the ability to control the read-only, archive, hidden, and system attributes of a file or a group of selected files. It also protects you from accidental deletion or replacement of a file by asking you to confirm such changes before they occur.

Changing File Attributes

To change the attributes of a file, select the file or files you want to affect, and then choose the Change Attributes command from the File menu. If you've selected more than one file, a dialog box appears asking whether you want to change the attributes of the files individually or all at the same time.

For actually changing the attributes, the Shell displays a dialog box in which you can select Hidden, System, Archive, Read Only, or any combination of these attributes. To change any attribute with the keyboard, press the Tab key to move the highlight to the attributes, use the Up or Down direction key to select the one you want, and then press the Spacebar to turn the attribute on or off. With the mouse, simply click on the attribute you want.

Confirming Deletions and Replacements

When you delete a file or a directory or when you are about to replace an existing file or directory with another file, the DOS Shell displays a dialog box that asks you to confirm the operation. If you don't want the Shell to ask you for approval every time, you can turn off this feature.

To control whether the Shell asks for confirmation before it deletes or replaces a file or directory, choose the Confirmation command from the Options menu. The Shell displays a dialog box titled File Options. Select Confirm On Delete, Confirm On Replace, Confirm On Mouse Operation, or all three, and then press Enter or click on OK.

COPYING, MOVING, AND FINDING FILES

Using the DOS Shell, you can copy one or more files in a single operation, even if they have unrelated names and extensions. You can also move files from one directory to another without having to use separate Copy and Erase commands.

Copying Files

To copy a file or a group of files, select one or more files from the file list, and then choose the Copy command from the File menu. The Shell displays a dialog box titled Copy File. The names of the files you selected appear in the From field. The name of the directory they are in appears in the To field. This is where you type the drive letter (if necessary) and path of the directory to which you want to copy the files. If you want, you can also specify a new name for a file you're copying. Press Enter or click on OK to carry out the command.

Moving Files

Moving files in the DOS Shell is the same as copying the files to their new location and then deleting the originals. Follow the same instructions you use for copying files, except choose the Move command from the File menu instead of the Copy command.

If you use a mouse, moving files is particularly easy. Simply select one or more files and drag them to the new directory.

Finding Files

Even the best intentions sometimes go astray. The same is true of files on a hard disk, especially one with a large number of files and directories on it. Finding one particular file on such a disk can become frustrating if you must scan one directory after another or type innumerable Directory commands.

From within the version 5 Shell, however, the search is easy. All you need is the Search command on the File menu. With this command, you can search the current directory or the entire disk, and you can search for a single file or a group of files you specify with wildcard characters. The search takes only a few seconds. If you search the entire disk, the command ends with a display of every file in every directory that matches the file name you specified.

THE PROGRAM LIST

A separate part of the Shell window, the Program List area is where the Shell displays the names of programs you can run. When the Shell is first installed, the Program List area displays a few standard items, usually including the names of the MS-DOS Editor, QBasic, and a group of programs called the Disk Utilities.

The Disk Utilities group includes a set of DOS commands related to managing your disks. One, Disk Copy, applies to diskettes only; three, Format, Quick Format, and Undelete, apply to both diskettes and hard disks; the two described here, Backup and Restore, work with hard disks only.

Using the Disk Utilities

If the Program List isn't displayed, choose Program/File Lists (to see both programs and files) or Program List (to see programs only) from the View menu. To use Backup, Restore, or one of the other disk utilities, highlight Disk Utilities and press Enter or double-click with the mouse.

The Shell displays the available choices, each of which you can now run from within the Shell.

Using the Backup Utility

To back up your hard disk, highlight Backup Fixed Disk and press Enter, or double-click on Backup Fixed Disk with your mouse. The Shell displays a dialog box titled Backup Fixed Disk. By default, the Shell backs up the entire contents of drive C, including all subdirectories, to drive A. To change the parameters of the Backup utility, edit the contents of the Parameters field in the Backup Fixed Disk dialog box. You can use the same options you use with the Backup command at the system prompt. When the command is as you want it, press Enter or click on OK. The backup utility prompts you to change diskettes when necessary.

Using the Restore Utility

To restore files that you previously backed up, highlight Restore Fixed Disk and press Enter or double-click with the mouse. The Shell displays a dialog box titled Restore Fixed Disk. Enter the source and destination, using any of the parameters you use with Restore from the system prompt. Press Enter or click on OK to start the Restore utility. Change backup diskettes if you're prompted to do so.

Returning to the Main Group

When you have finished your work in the Disk Utilities group, you can press Esc to return to the Main Group (the original list of programs). If you are using a mouse, double-click on Main at the top of the Disk Utilities list.

Personalizing the Shell

In your work with the Shell, you can define your own program groups. You can, for example, define a group named Word Processing. Within this group, you can include your word processor and related items, such as programs that check your grammar and spelling. Similarly, you can include your spreadsheet, tax, and other financial programs in a group named Finance. If you want to restrict access to a particular group, such as your financial programs, the Shell even lets you assign a password that must be entered before the application will start.

Using groups to organize your programs is similar to using directories to organize the files on your hard disk. Like directories, such groups can help you visualize the work you do and the way certain tasks are related to one another.

As a hard disk user, you should be aware of your ability to create program groups, add programs to the Program List, and define the ways in which they behave. The details are outside the strict focus of this quick reference and are not covered here, but the procedure is not difficult. If you want to experiment, begin by selecting the Program List area. When you do, the menus at the top of the screen undergo a subtle change, as you can see by opening the File menu. Instead of the many file-management commands you see when the File List area is active, the File menu now offers a smaller group of commands that let you tailor the Program List to your own needs. To add a program or a program group to the list, you use the New command. To define the way a program behaves, you use the Properties command, also on the File menu. Your documentation should provide all the additional information you need, as will the Shell's online Help.

Once you've tailored the Program List area to your satisfaction, you can start more than one of your applications and switch from one to another without quitting each program. To do this, choose Enable Task Swapper from the Options menu. To move from the Shell to a particular program, choose its name from the Active Task List. To move from one active program to another, hold down the Alt key, press Tab until the name of the program is displayed, and then release the Alt key. To cycle through the active programs, press Alt-Esc. To return to the Shell, press Ctrl-Esc.

LEAVING THE SHELL

If you want to exit the DOS Shell and return to the system prompt, choose the Exit command from the File menu or press either F3 or Alt-F4. You can return to the Shell at any time simply by typing *dosshell*.

Index